Let Them Eat Kale!

Simple and Delicious Recipes for Everyone's Favorite Superfood

Julia Mueller

SKYHORSE PUBLISHING

Skyhorse Publishing books may be purchased in bulk at special discounts for sales promotion, corporate gifts, fund-raising, or educational purposes. Special editions can also be created to specifications. For details, contact the Special Sales Department, Skyhorse Publishing, 307 West 36th Street, 11th Floor, New York, NY 10018 or info@skyhorsepublishing.com.

Skyhorse® and Skyhorse Publishing® are registered trademarks of Skyhorse Publishing, Inc.®, a Delaware corporation.

Visit our website at www.skyhorsepublishing.com.

10 9 8 7 6 5 4 3 2

Library of Congress Cataloging-in-Publication Data

Mueller, Julia, author.
 Let them eat kale! : simple and delicious recipes for everyone's favorite superfood / Julia Mueller.
     pages cm
 Summary: "Kale is considered one of the world's most powerful superfoods for very good reasons. It's packed with antioxidants, which help neutralize free radicals in the body, which, in turn, helps to prevent many kinds of cancer. Just one cup provides more than 100 percent of the daily value of vitamins A, C, and K, and it's low calorie, high in fiber, and fat-free. Furthermore, kale is high in iron and has a good dose of omega-3 fatty acids, which work as an anti-inflammatory and help fight arthritis, asthma, and autoimmune disorders. And to top all that off, author Julia Mueller proves that it can be delicious"-- Provided by publisher.
 ISBN 978-1-62914-189-3 (hardback)
 1. Cooking (Kale) I. Title.
 TX803.G74M84 2014
 641.6'5347--dc23
                              2014000267

Printed in China

This book is dedicated to G.D.

Contents

Introduction

When I first discovered kale, I was very unsure of what to do with it. *Why is it so tough? And bitter? What do I do with the stem? Should I punish the people I dislike with it? Why would one* do *kale to herself?* In spite of my misgivings, I was intrigued. I knew, based on the huge number of both kale lovers and kale naysayers popping up everywhere, there was something there. And that something was beneficial to my health.

I warmed up to kale by incorporating it into my go-to vegetable stir-fry and scrambled eggs. As my love for kale grew, I began experimenting with it in ways that compliment it, as opposed to simply hiding it. While I continue to "hide" kale in my smoothies, soups, and salsas, I also enjoy it in the frontlines of a recipe. I'm 200 percent serious when I say I make all of my salads with kale, as it has become my preference over all forms of greenery. Move over, iceberg lettuce, let kale reign!

Amidst the growing whole food trend, kale has exploded in popularity. But beyond merely being trendy, the leafy green is valuable both from culinary and health standpoints. Those who love kale understand it can be prepared in an appetizing way and rejoice in its health benefits. Those who hate it aren't wild about its flavor and texture, and would prefer to take a swift kick to the gut than see another kale salad recipe.

Just like all things in life, kale should be approached with an open mind and fresh perspective. We can acknowledge that unlike cheese, kale needs a little attention before it becomes delicious. We can moderate our intake of kale so that we don't go into hyper-kale-trend burnout. And just because kale is swell doesn't mean we need to make cocktails or brownies out of it. We can take kale for what it is—a tough, fibrous vegetable that is virtually unchewable in its raw form—and turn it into something tasty and nutritious.

In developing the recipes in this book, I have taken a realistic approach to kale. I wasn't always a kale lover. I don't eat kale every day, and I understand that it has a specific place in cooking. For me, that place is not cake. Nor is it cookies. Nor will you catch me sipping a kale-infused vodka tonic. There are boundaries. In this book, you will find healthful recipes that are practical, affordable, approachable to make any night of the week, and absolutely delicious. For the seasoned kale lover, the kale newby, or even the kale-averse, this book contains recipes that anyone can prepare easily and enjoy bountifully.

Why do I love kale enough to write an entire cookbook on it? The answer is twofold. I enjoy creating dishes that expand culinary pallets, and it is the least expensive health insurance policy I know of. 'Tis true: when prepared well, kale is absolutely fabulous both in flavor and texture, and it is one of the most nutritious foods you can put in your body. Before jettisoning you into the wonderful world of kale recipes, I have provided information about the health benefits of kale, methods of preparing it, gardening tips, cautionary notes, and other tidbits of information.

Stay. Enjoy. Eat well, eat often!

Why Kale is Queen:

Kale is one of the most nutrient-dense superfoods in the world. By definition, superfoods contain a high concentration of vitamins, minerals, and antioxidants, are low in calories, boost immunity, and are disease-fighting. Kale is a part of the cruciferous vegetable family (Brassicaceae), which also includes cauliflower, bok choy, cabbage, broccoli, and Brussels sprouts.

Kale sports high concentrations of Vitamins K, A, and C, beta-carotene, and phytonutrients. Just one cup of chopped kale earns you 684% of your daily value of Vitamin K, 206% of Vitamin A, and 134% of Vitamin C.[1] These three measurements, on top of kale's reputation for fighting cancer, are what compose the leafy green's wow-factor. Let's look at these nutrients closer to really show her royalty.

All of that Vitamin K helps your blood clot normally, strengthens your bones, and prevents bone loss as you age. Additionally, it helps cleanse the liver and protects against prostate and liver cancers.[2] Part of the reason kale has become more popular than collard greens or spinach is because it contains more Vitamin K than other leafy greens. Does this mean one should *replace* other leafy greens with kale? Absolutely not. Regardless of kale's incredible health benefits, maintaining variety in your diet is very important.

Vitamins A and C and phytonutrients are antioxidants, which help prevent oxidation and damage to your cells. Because cancer has been linked to excessive amounts of oxidation, antioxidants may help reduce the risk of cancer, as well as fight it. Numerous studies have shown there is a connection between diets high in antioxidants and low onset of cancer and disease. The nutrient qualities in kale may lower the risk of ovary, breast, colon, prostate, and bladder cancers. Antioxidants also help keep your blood healthy and prevent inflammation throughout your cells and body.[3] Detoxification is important in order to keep your cells fully functional, reduce tissue damage, and keep your blood clean.

Exposure to pollution and chemicals, as well as other unnatural substances we consume and ingest, make antioxidants and detoxifying vital for staying healthy.

Kale is full of phytonutrients, including forty-five different types of flavonoids, beta-carotene (and other carotenoids), glucosinolates, sulfurophane, and kaempferol. In general, phytonutrients help support your immune system and prevent disease. More specifically, beta-carotene and flavonoids are known for their antioxidant qualities, and glucosinolates have been pegged as a cancer-fighter. Sulfurophane is an excellent detoxer, and kaempferol activates specific genes that promote longevity. Essentially, these phytonutrients keep you at a safe distance from the doctor's office.[4]

Kale also contains manganese, copper, calcium, potassium, and iron. These minerals are also antioxidants. They help maintain a balanced blood sugar level, strengthen your bones and connective tissue, lower cholesterol, and help your body break down fatty acids.[5]

All things considered, I view kale as an incredibly affordable preventative medicine technique. It may lower the risk of heart disease and many types of cancers. Kale helps prevent obesity, regulates bowel movements, and boosts the immune system. All of its vitamins and nutrient qualities support your brain and serve as proof that you are what you eat! Ultimately, this simple leafy green is one of the means to a long, healthy life.

With all of that said, it is important to be realistic about where kale stands relative to other vegetables. Is it incredibly nutritious? Yes. Should you toss other vegetables out the window because they don't measure up? No, don't do that. While dense, the health benefits of kale are not the only source, and are not a cure-all to medical ailments. Be curious about your health, experiment, and above all, enjoy the food you eat.

Types of Kale

There are many varieties of kale, but the two most commonly found in your grocery store are green curly kale and Dinosaur (also known as dino, lacinato, or Tuscan) kale. Depending on your local market, you can also find red curly kale, Asian kale, or baby kale, all of which you can use for any of the recipes in this book. Below is a list of characteristics and descriptions of the varieties of kale.

Curly Kale

Curly kale looks exactly how it sounds: the leaves are tight, curly, and springy. Curly kale comes in multiple colors, but the kind you will come across the most at your grocery store is bright green. You will also see this kale less commonly in a pale light green hue, green with red or purple tips, and entirely red (which looks more purple than red).

While this kale may be the most popular, I find it also to be the most difficult to work with raw. For that reason, I suggest massaging curly kale with lemon juice for raw applications, or using it in your cooked meals. Curly kale has a peppery and somewhat bitter flavor when left raw.

Dinosaur (Dino, Lacinato, Tuscan) Kale

Dinosaur kale is also frequently called dino, lacinato, or Tuscan kale. The leaves are long, dark green, and resemble dinosaur skin. Dino kale is my favorite kale to use in salads because I like that I can chop it into strips, making it easier to manage than curly kale. Its flavor tends to be less bitter than other kinds of kale, and it is easier to chew in its raw form than other kale varieties.

Russian Red Kale

With a purple stem and flat green leaves, Russian red kale is a beautiful leafy green, although it can be difficult to find this variety in the grocery store. The leaves of Russian red kale are much more tender and sweeter than other types of kale. It requires slightly less time to cook and can be quite tasty its raw form.

Baby Kale

Baby kale tends to come packaged in a plastic container. It is convenient for making salads, as there is no chopping involved, and because the leaves are young, they are more tender and less fibrous than adult kale leaves. Baby kale can come as a variety of two or more types of kale, or it can come as one

type of kale, depending on the farmer's crop. Although baby kale is perfect for using in salads, it is also great for sautéing or putting in soups. Just like adult kale leaves, baby kale can be incorporated into any of the recipes in this book.

Methods for Preparing Kale:

Although raw or unprepared kale has the reputation of being bitter and fibrous, there are numerous ways of softening the flavor and texture of kale. Below is a list of ways one can prepare kale. Just as you would any other vegetable, wash kale in cold water prior to cooking or consuming it. While raw vegetables are very healthful, the health benefits of kale are easier for your body to absorb after it has been cooked. Cooking kale for 3 to 5 minutes is all it takes to make those unrelenting fibers softer and more approachable for your body to digest.

Blanching

Blanching is a quick way of cooking food (typically a vegetable) by dunking the ingredient in boiling water, allowing it to cook for a specific period of time, and then immediately plunging the ingredient in an ice bath. Some people like to blanch kale before using it in salads because it reduces the bitter flavor. You can also blanch kale prior to adding it to a hot recipe, which can be a quicker method of cooking the kale than adding it to the recipe and waiting for it to soften.

1. Bring a full pot of water to a boil and have a large bowl of ice water ready.
2. Add the kale leaves (with stems still attached) to the boiling water and allow them to cook about 30 seconds.
3. Using tongs, pull the leaves out and immediately place them in the ice bath. Allow the leaves to chill for just a few seconds, scoop them out, and add them to your recipe. You can also toss the blanched kale in salt, pepper, olive oil, and lemon juice for an easy, healthful side dish.

   Note: you can skip the ice bath altogether and place the blanched leaves in a colander so they can cool and drain.

Braising

A cooking method that requires both "dry" and "wet" heat is known as braising. The food is seared on a skillet, then placed in a pot with liquid in order to finish the cooking process. Braising tends to be a "slow and low" cooking technique. Sautéing kale leaves with olive oil, garlic, onion, salt, and pepper, then adding chicken or vegetable broth to cook off, is an easy and tasty way to braise kale.

1. Sauté your ingredients to desired level of "doneness." If using onion, sauté until fragrant and translucent, about 8 to 10 minutes.
2. Add the kale leaves and continue sautéing 2 minutes.
3. Add a small amount of broth or water.
4. Bring the mixture to a boil and cook until all of the liquid has evaporated.

Sautéing

Adding oil, vegetables, and/or meat to a skillet (or wok) and stirring them until cooked is a food preparation method known as sautéing. Stir-frying involves the same steps as sautéing, although it is typically performed at a higher temperature. Sautéeing or stir-frying vegetables is a fairly fast and very tasty way of preparing vegetables.

Add kale to your vegetable sauté or stir-frying to inject a great deal of health benefits to your meal. Because kale requires less time to cook than most other vegetables, add it to your sauté after everything else has finished cooking, allowing it to steam until softened and wilted.

1. Heat oil in a skillet or wok and heat to medium or medium-high.
2. Add ingredients, beginning with those that require more time to cook—onions, potatoes, turnips, carrots, celery, etc.—followed by the ingredients that require less time to cook.
3. Sauté, stirring regularly, until all ingredients are at the desired level of doneness.
4. Add chopped kale leaves, cover the skillet/wok, and allow the leaves to steam on

top of the other vegetables until they turn bright green and are soft, about 3 to 4 minutes.

5. Stir the kale leaves into the other ingredients and serve.

Roasting

Roasting involves baking ingredients in the oven for a specific period of time. Roasting vegetables is a great way of cultivating flavor and texture, and is my preference over steamed vegetables. Roasting requires more time than any other method of food preparation. It is less common to roast kale with other vegetables than it is to roast kale by itself to make crispy kale chips.

1. Preheat your oven to roasting temperature (typically between 350 and 375 degrees F.).
2. Add chopped vegetables and kale to a casserole dish.
3. Drizzle vegetables with oil, salt, pepper, and other spices.
4. Roast until all vegetables are cooked through, stirring once or twice. Roasting can require anywhere between 45 and 60 minutes, depending on the size of the chopped vegetables and the amount of vegetables in the casserole dish. Note that kale cooks fairly quickly, so make sure the leaves are coated in enough oil so that they don't burn.
5. Remove the vegetables from the oven and serve along with your favorite main dish.

Grilling

Grilling is a great way of cooking kale in the summertime, when you are already grilling meat and vegetables. It adds crispy texture and charred barbecue flavor to the leaves, and is perfect for adding to any rustic dish. Grilled kale salads are delicious, especially when grilled kale leaves are combined with other grilled vegetables and dressed in a sauce or vinaigrette.

1. Rinse kale leaves well and pat them dry.
2. Lightly brush each leaf with canola, coconut, or grapeseed oil (or high temperature oil of choice), making sure both sides of the leaves are coated.
3. Sprinkle each leaf with salt and pepper and add other spices if desired.
4. Place on a hot grill and allow leaves to cook 30 seconds to 1 minute on each side, just until browned and softened.
5. You can either chop the leaves, discarding the stems, and add the leaves to your dish, or you can keep the leaves whole and serve them as a rustic salad or side dish.

Dehydrating

Dehydrating fruits, vegetables, and meats removes or evaporates moisture out of food, which gives it a great concentration of flavor and a longer shelf life than fresh food. Those who own a dehydrator can make excellent crispy kale chips, although kale chips can be made in the oven as well.

1. Rinse a whole head of kale in cool water and pat leaves dry.
2. Tear large pieces of the leaves off the stems (discard stems or save for later).
3. Place leaves on your dehydrator trays and sprinkle with salt (and other seasonings, if desired).
4. Turn your dehydrator on to 115 degrees F and dehydrate for 4 to 5 hours or until desired crispiness is achieved.
5. Note: As an alternative, you can place your dehydrator at 140 degrees F for 1 hour and then lower the temperature to around 115 for an additional hour. If you choose this method, the chips will no longer be considered "raw" once they reach a temperature above 120 degrees F.

Massaged

Massaging kale with lemon juice is an excellent technique for breaking down some of its fibrousness and making it more palatable for salads. Simply massaging lemon juice into kale leaves is an efficient way of keeping kale raw, while making it easier to consume.

1. Thoroughly rinse the kale under cool water and pat dry.
2. Remove the stems and discard or save for later use.
3. Finely chop the kale leaves and place them in a serving bowl.
4. Drizzle lemon juice over the leaves and use your hands to massage the juice into the leaves until they have softened and turned dark. Allow the kale to sit 10 to 15 minutes in order to maximize the effects of the lemon juice.
5. Add desired ingredients to the salad, toss with your favorite salad dressing, and serve.

Raw

Leaving kale raw and unmassaged is the least popular way of consuming it. When left raw, kale is difficult to chew, has a somewhat astringent quality to it, and tastes bitter. It is also more difficult to digest than cooked kale. For this reason, I prefer cooking kale, or massaging it for salads. When leaving kale raw, it best to use any kale except curly kale, as the flat leaves are easier to chew than curly ones.

1. Rinse kale very well under cool water.
2. Pat kale dry or set in a colander to drain the water off.

3. Remove the stems from the kale leaves and either discard them or save them to use later.
4. Finely chop the leaves and add them to other raw ingredients.

Kale and Fat
In order to properly digest highly vitamin-rich fibrous vegetables, one must also consume fat in some form. Without fat, many vitamins and minerals are not as effectively absorbed into your system. Cruciferous vegetables are more difficult for your digestive system to break down than noncruciferous vegetables, so it is important to be mindful of consuming these veggies in conjunction with fat in order to maintain a happy digestive system. Kale is very calorie-light (one cup of chopped kale leaves contains only 30 to 40 calories) and contains almost no fat. You will find the recipes in this book contain an ample level of fat through oils, meats, dairy products, coconut milk, and nuts. This way, you can enjoy a flavorful and delicious meal, as well as reap the full benefits of its nutrient quality.

What to do With Kale Stems
While kale stems do not contain the same vitamin density as kale leaves, they can still be used in your cooking. The stems contain a great deal of fiber and can be added to smoothies, or chopped and added to sautéed vegetables or even scrambled eggs. While most people are not excited at the prospect of eating kale stems, it remains an option if you prefer to maintain a no-waste household.

Sourcing Your Kale
The optimal way of sourcing your kale would be to either grow it yourself (it's easy, I swear!), or to buy it from your local farmer's market. Small farms grow a wide variety of vegetables, which ensures you're not eating the same exact type of kale each and every time you prepare it. This helps to not only maintain variety in your diet but also ensures you don't get bored of using the same vegetable over and over in your cooking.

Of course, not everyone has the luxury of growing kale at home or has access to a farmer's market due to location and climate. Most grocery stores carry one or more varieties of kale. I always, *always* recommend buying organic kale. Inorganically grown leafy greens hold pesticides, which are almost impossible to wash off.

Tips for Gardening Kale
Growing your own kale organically is an affordable way of sourcing your greens—not to mention, harvesting your own food is fun! Kale is one of the few vegetables that can

be harvested multiple times throughout the growing season. Once the leaves grow to desired size, trim them off and use them in your recipes. New leaves will grow and you can get at least three harvests out of your kale, depending on the length of your growing season. Note that you don't have to wait long in order to trim your kale—the smaller leaves are more tender than the larger leaves, so grow your kale according to taste.

While some people prefer using seedling transplants for growing kale, it is one of the easier vegetables to grow from seed. In this sense, you can skip the step of growing your own kale seedlings, or save money on purchasing them, as using seed is the easiest and most affordable way of growing your own kale. There is nothing like harvesting your own vegetables that you have grown yourself from start to finish!

Kale is a winter vegetable, meaning it is best when grown in colder climates. In fact, kale tastes sweeter when it is grown at colder temperatures. For areas where the weather stays fairly warm (above 15 degrees F) in the winter, fall is a great time to plant. For areas that have winters that consistently bring in freezes, it is best to plant kale in the springtime, 3 to 4 weeks before the last frost. Kale can grow at a soil temperature as low as 20 degrees F. and up to 80 degrees F. The warmer the climate, the more bitter and fibrous the kale will be.

Depending on the temperature of the soil and the type of kale you're growing, it will take between 45 and 60 days between planting and harvest. When growing kale during the winter months, it is best to harvest it just after the first frost of the season. A small amount of frost will not ruin the plants and will actually make them taste better. Remember, as soon as the leaves grow to the desired size, you may trim them off and use them, making room for more leaves to grow.

Although kale plants will still grow in partially shady areas, they love direct sunlight. It is best to plant seeds (or seedlings) in an area that gets at least 6 or more hours of direct sunlight per day. Dig small holes about 3 inches deep and plant seeds or seedlings. Space the seeds 18 to 24 inches apart. The more space each plant has, the larger the leaves will grow.

Use good quality soil and/or compost for growing your kale to ensure it has the nutrients it needs to thrive. Don't be surprised if you find small holes (created by worms) or aphids on your kale leaves. As long as the leaves aren't overly damaged, they are still useable, but be sure to soak the leaves well before cooking with them. Bug infestations are a sign that your kale plants are past their harvesting prime. Avoid allowing your kale to become overgrown, and if desired, use organic sprays to keep the bugs away.

Kale loves water. It is best to keep the soil moist, not allowing it to fully dry out between waterings. In my experience, it is difficult to "overwater" kale, as it will enjoy 1" to 1.5" of water per week. Kale is one of the easier plants to grow because it is not incredibly sensitive to too much or too little water.

Kale Cautions

It is not recommended for those who are on blood thinners or related clotting medication to eat kale due to its high concentration of Vitamin K. Because Vitamin K helps naturally clot blood, it can weaken the effects of anti-clotting medication. Kale also contains oxalates, which have been known to cause kidney and gall stones when consumed in large volumes. In addition, kale contains goitrogens, which prevent iron absorption and may worsen the symptoms of hypothyroidism. Goitrogens are denatured when cooked, so those who have thyroid problems should simply avoid eating raw kale.[6]

Endnotes

[1] Zelman, Kathleen M., MPH, RD, LD. "The Truth About Kale." *Web MD*. N.p., n.d. Web. 29 Dec. 2013. <http://www.webmd.com/food-recipes/features/the-truth-about-kale>.

[2] "Vitamin K." *The World's Healthiest Foods*. N.p., n.d. Web. 1 Dec. 2013. <http://www.whfoods.com/genpage.php?tname=nutrient&dbid=112>.

[3] "Phytonutrients." *Web MD*. N.p., n.d. Web. 29 Dec. 2013. <http://www.webmd.com/diet/phyto-nutrients-faq>.

[4] Ramsey, Drew, M.D. "This Is Your Brain on Kale." *Huffpost Healthy Living*. N.p., 2 July 2013. Web. 29 Dec. 2013. <http://www.huffingtonpost.com/drew-ramsey-md/health-benefits-kale_b_3529768.html>.

[5] "Manganese." *The World's Healthiest Foods*. N.p., n.d. Web. 1 Dec. 2013. <http://www.whfoods.com/genpage.php?tname=nutrient&dbid=77>.

[6] Daniels, Chris. "Greens, Kale & Thyroid Problems." *Livestrong*. N.p., 12 Oct. 2013. Web. 15 Dec. 2013. <http://www.livestrong.com/article/519961-greens-kale-thyroid-problems/>.

Breakfast

Blueberry Superfood Smoothie

Makes smoothies for 2.

INSTRUCTIONS:

Add all ingredients to a blender, starting with the liquids (this will help blend everything together).

Blend until smooth.

INGREDIENTS:

1 cup kale leaves, loosely packed

1½ frozen bananas

1 cup frozen blueberries

¼ cup coconut milk (full-fat from the can)

1½ cups almond milk

Chorizo, Potato, and Kale Hash

Serves 4.

INSTRUCTIONS:

1. In a large skillet, heat oil to medium and add the chopped yam.
2. Sauté for 3 to 5 minutes before adding the red onion. Continue to sauté until veggies are softened, about 10 minutes.
3. Add the ground chorizo and continue sautéing until chorizo is cooked all the way through, about 5 minutes.
4. Add the chopped kale leaves and cover skillet to allow kale to soften and cook.
5. Once wilted, stir kale into the hash and serve with over-easy, fried, or poached eggs on top!

INGREDIENTS:

2 tablespoons olive oil
2 cups jewel yam, chopped
   into ½" pieces*
1½ cups chopped red onion
½ pound ground turkey or
   chicken chorizo
4 cups tightly packed chopped
   Russian red kale
Eggs for serving

*You can also use russet or red
   potatoes.

While breakfast hashes are typically chock-full of greasy bacon or sausage and potatoes, I love making hashes using leaner chorizos, such as ground turkey or chicken chorizo. Replacing russet potatoes with yams or sweet potatoes and adding kale makes this breakfast a healthier alternative to your typical hash. You can also use this hash to make breakfast burritos and tacos, or an omelet.

Green Apple Ginger Smoothie

Makes one large smoothie.

INSTRUCTIONS:

1. Add all ingredients to a high-powered blender and blend until a uniform consistency is achieved.
2. Test the smoothie for taste and add honey as necessary.
3. For a creamier (less gritty) consistency, add one frozen banana to the recipe.

INGREDIENTS:

1 green apple, cored and chopped

2 handfuls kale leaves

2 teaspoons fresh ginger, peeled and grated

1 tablespoon honey

½ cup coconut milk

½ cup almond milk

This green apple smoothie with ginger is full of nutrients and flavor! The texture of the kale and apple results in a somewhat gritty smoothie, so I would caution that the recipe as stated above should be for seasoned green smoothie drinkers only. If you're new to green smoothies, you can achieve a creamier texture by adding a frozen banana, if desired. This simple smoothie is perfect for a detox or for simply adding vitamins to your daily diet.

Huevos Rancheros Bake

Serves 4.

INSTRUCTIONS:

1. Preheat your oven to 350 degrees F.
2. In a large skillet, heat the oil to medium and add the chopped onion.
3. Sauté, stirring consistently, until onion is translucent, about 8 minutes. Add the garlic and sauté another 2 minutes. Add the kale, black beans, and chopped tortillas, and continue sautéing until the kale is bright green and softened, about 5 minutes.
4. Divide the veggie mixture between four ramekins.
5. Make a small well in the center of the veggies for each ramekin and carefully crack an egg into each well.
6. Place ramekins on a baking sheet and bake for 20 to 25 minutes, or until the egg whites set up.
7. Serve with shredded cheese and avocado.

INGREDIENTS:

1 tablespoon olive oil

1 yellow onion, chopped

3 cloves garlic, minced

1 head kale, chopped

1 14-ounce can black beans, drained and rinsed

3 to 4 corn tortillas, chopped into bite sizes

2 cups of your favorite salsa

4 eggs

Avocado and cheddar cheese for serving

I can put away Mexican food every single day of the week, and that includes eating it for breakfast. Huevos rancheros is one of my favorite breakfast items, and I like to lighten it up and add nutrition by incorporating homemade salsa, black beans, and kale. To take the fun a step further, you can bake your huevos in the oven instead of scrambling or frying it on the stovetop.

Mango Matcha Green Tea Smoothie

Makes smoothies for 2.

INSTRUCTIONS:

Add all ingredients to a blender and blend until completely smooth. Add more liquid as necessary to get everything blended.

INGREDIENTS:

1½ ripe bananas, frozen

1 cup ripe mango, chopped

1 cup tightly packed kale leaves

2 teaspoons to 1 tablespoon matcha green tea powder

1½ cups unsweetened almond milk

Matcha green tea is packed full of antioxidants! Combining matcha with kale and delicious mango and banana makes for an incredibly flavorful and nutrient-rich smoothie.

Orange Creamsicle Kale Stem Smoothie

Makes smoothies for 2.

INSTRUCTIONS:

1. Peel the navel oranges and separate the sections.
2. Chop the kale stalks in half or quarters.
3. Add all ingredients to a blender and blend until smooth.

INGREDIENTS:

4 small (or 2 large) ripe navel oranges, peeled

Zest of 1 orange

2 frozen bananas

1 cup full-fat coconut milk

½ cup unsweetened almond milk

4 kale stems

3 ice cubes

If you enjoy orange creamsicle popsicles, you'll love this smoothie! It bears close resemblance to the popsicle, but is full of nutrition, and a perfect way to start the day. While most people throw away kale stems, there are many uses for them! I like to put them in my smoothies in order to add fiber and vitamins and to avoid waste. While kale stems are fairly gritty, blending them well with other ingredients makes the texture nearly undetectable.

Peach and Kale Stem Smoothie

Makes smoothies for 2.

INSTRUCTIONS:

Add all ingredients to a blender and blend until smooth. If necessary, add more almond milk or juice to help the blender process the frozen fruit.

INGREDIENTS:

2 ripe peaches, pitted and frozen

2 ripe bananas, peeled and frozen

2 kale stems

1 teaspoon fresh ginger, peeled and grated

8 ice cubes

½ cup almond milk

¾ cup orange juice

¼ cup coconut milk (full-fat from the can)

Pear Avocado Ginger Smoothie

Makes 2 thick smoothies.

INSTRUCTIONS:

Add all ingredients to a high-powered blender and blend until smooth.

Note: Add additional almond milk for thinner consistency.

INGREDIENTS:

1 ripe Bartlett pear, stem
   removed, chopped

1 frozen banana

1 cup tightly packed kale
   leaves

½ avocado

1 teaspoon fresh ginger, finely
   grated

3 ice cubes

½ cup almond milk

1 cup vanilla yogurt

If you've never tried an avocado smoothie, the idea may seem foreign or downright disgusting to you. Ripe avocados add nutrients and a creamy texture to smoothies, making them healthful and tasty. The ginger and pear add a sweetness and a little heat making this smoothie flavorful with a very pleasing thick consistency.

Piña Colada Smoothie

Makes smoothies for 2.

INSTRUCTIONS:

Add all ingredients to a high-powered blender and blend until completely smooth.

INGREDIENTS:

2 bananas

1 cup pineapple chunks

2 cups kale leaves

1 cup coconut milk

1 cup pineapple juice

2 cups ice

You'd never know there is kale in this smoothie! It tastes just like a piña colada, minus the alcohol. Coconut milk and pineapple juice are both full of health benefits, and of course the kale gives this smoothie a vitamin boost.

Poached Egg over Sautéed Kale

Serves 2.

INSTRUCTIONS:

1. In order to poach eggs, fill a saucepan or pot with water and heat just until it's about ready to boil. Add 1 tablespoon of white vinegar, then carefully crack an egg into the water. You can use a slotted spoon to carefully push the egg white closer to the yolk, so that the egg stays somewhat together. Allow the egg to sit about 4 minutes in the hot water.

2. Carefully lift the egg out of the water with the slotted spoon and place it on a plate. Repeat for desired amount of eggs.

3. In a large skillet, heat oil to medium. Add the chopped kale leaves and sauté, stirring to coat the leaves with oil. Cover the skillet and allow the leaves and stem to soften, about 3 to 4 minutes.

4. Serve sautéed kale with poached egg, avocado, salsa, and other desired toppings.

INGREDIENTS:

1 tablespoon olive oil

1 head of kale, stems removed, leaves chopped

2 to 4 eggs, poached

Salt and pepper to taste

Avocado and salsa for serving

Sausage and Kale Scramble

INSTRUCTIONS:

1. Heat oil in a medium skillet. Add the chopped potato and sauté, stirring every few minutes until it begins to soften, about 8 to 10 minutes.
2. Add the ground sausage and brown the meat, chopping it into bite sizes using a spatula.
3. Add the green onion and kale leaves and cover the pan, allowing the kale to soften, about 2 minutes.
4. In a bowl, whisk together the eggs. Pour the eggs uniformly over the sausage mixture. Allow the eggs to sit and cook a few minutes before flipping them over (this ensures the contents of your scramble hold together).
5. Sprinkle the cheese over the eggs and continue cooking until eggs are cooked through and cheese is melted.
6. Season the eggs to taste with salt and pepper. Serve with guacamole and sour cream or plain yogurt.

INGREDIENTS:

1 tablespoon olive oil

2 cups white sweet potato (or red potato), chopped into ½" pieces

1 cup ground turkey breakfast sausage (or breakfast sausage of choice)

½ cup green onion, chopped

2 cups tightly packed green kale, leaves chopped

6 eggs, lightly beaten

½ cup mozzarella or jack cheese, grated

Salt and pepper to taste

Savory Cheesy Kale Pancakes

Makes 15 pancakes.

INSTRUCTIONS:

1. Heat the oil to medium in a skillet and add the onion. Sauté until onion is translucent, about 8 minutes.
2. Add the garlic and sauté 2 minutes.
3. Add the chopped kale leaves and sauté, stirring constantly until leaves have wilted and softened, about 3 minutes.
4. Remove skillet from heat and set aside.
5. In a mixing bowl, combine the oat flour, shredded cheese, baking powder, baking soda, and salt. In a separate bowl, whisk together the eggs and almond milk.
6. Pour the egg/milk mixture into the mixing bowl with the dry ingredients and stir to combine. Add the sautéed kale/onion mixture to the pancake batter and fold into the batter until combined.
7. Heat a large skillet or griddle to medium and add just enough oil to lightly coat the surface of the pan. Using a measuring cup, measure ¼ cup of the batter and pour it into the skillet. Cook until the sides of the pancakes firm and centers plump up, about 2 minutes. Flip the pancakes and cook an additional 2 minutes, or until the pancakes are cooked through.
8. Serve hot with your favorite breakfast foods, such as eggs, sausage, or bacon.

INGREDIENTS:

1 tablespoon olive oil

⅓ cup yellow onion, finely chopped

6 cloves garlic, minced

4 cups curly green kale, leaves finely chopped

1½ cups oat flour*

1 cup gouda cheese, shredded

2 teaspoons baking powder

¼ teaspoon baking soda

½ teaspoon salt

3 eggs, lightly beaten

1⅓ cups unsweetened almond milk

*If you are gluten-intolerant, make sure your oat flour is gluten-free, or grind your own gluten-free oats into flour.

Superfood Breakfast Tacos

Serves 5 to 6.

INSTRUCTIONS:

1. In a large skillet, heat the oil to just above medium. Sauté onion and sweet potato until sweet potato is al dente and onion is softened, about 15 minutes. If necessary, add a few tablespoons of water periodically in order to help steam the sweet potato.

2. Crack the eggs into a bowl, add the spices and salt, and whisk to scramble. Set aside. Remove the stems on the kale leaves and chop the leaves.

3. Wrap the tortillas in aluminum foil and put them in the oven at 350 degrees F until they're hot, about 7 minutes.

4. Heat the can of black beans in a saucepan over medium-low heat.

5. Once the sweet potatoes are cooked to desired level of "doneness," add the kale leaves and mix in. Allow kale leaves to soften, about 45 seconds.

6. Pour eggs evenly over the veggies and cook for 1 minute. Using a spatula, flip the eggs/veggies over on top of themselves so that everything stays clumped together. Cook about 2 minutes. Repeat several times until eggs are cooked all the way.

7. Time to prepare your tacos! Remove the tortillas from the aluminum foil, sprinkle them with cheese, then add black beans, scrambled eggs/veggies, and top with diced tomato and avocado. Enjoy your filling, nutritious breakfast!

INGREDIENTS:

2 tablespoons olive oil

2 cups sweet potato (peel on), chopped into ½" pieces

½ yellow onion, chopped

1 14-ounce can black beans

4 cups tightly packed kale leaves, chopped

9 eggs

½ teaspoon turmeric

1 teaspoon ground cumin

1 teaspoon garlic powder

Salt to taste

For serving: Corn or flour tortillas

Avocado

Tomato

Cheese

Zucchini, Kale, and Sage Frittata

Serves 6.

INSTRUCTIONS:

1. Shred the zucchini and place it in a fine strainer. Placing the strainer on top of a bowl or over the sink, use your hands to squeeze the water out of the zucchini. It's okay if you don't squeeze all of the water out, but try to get the majority of it. Set shredded zucchini aside.
2. Preheat oven to 350 degrees F.
3. Heat olive oil in a 10" to 12" cast-iron (or oven-safe) skillet.
4. Add chopped kale leaves and stir until kale begins to soften. Cover the skillet to allow kale to cook and soften, about 1 to 2 minutes.
5. Add the green onion and chopped sage and sauté another minute or two. Remove from heat and allow the greens to cool completely.
6. In a mixing bowl, beat the eggs. Stir in the shredded zucchini, salt, and cheese. Pour in the green mixture and mix everything well.
7. Pour the egg and veggie mixture into the same skillet you were using to sauté the greens, making sure the mixture is evenly distributed.
8. Place the skillet in the oven and bake for 15 to 18 minutes or until cooked all the way through.

INGREDIENTS:

2 tablespoons olive oil

3 cups tightly packed kale leaves, chopped

5 stalks green onion, chopped

¼ to ⅓ cup loosely packed sage (or basil) leaves, chopped

2 cups zucchini, shredded (1 large or 2 small zucchini squash)

½ teaspoon salt

12 eggs, lightly beaten

½ cup jack cheese (or cheddar)

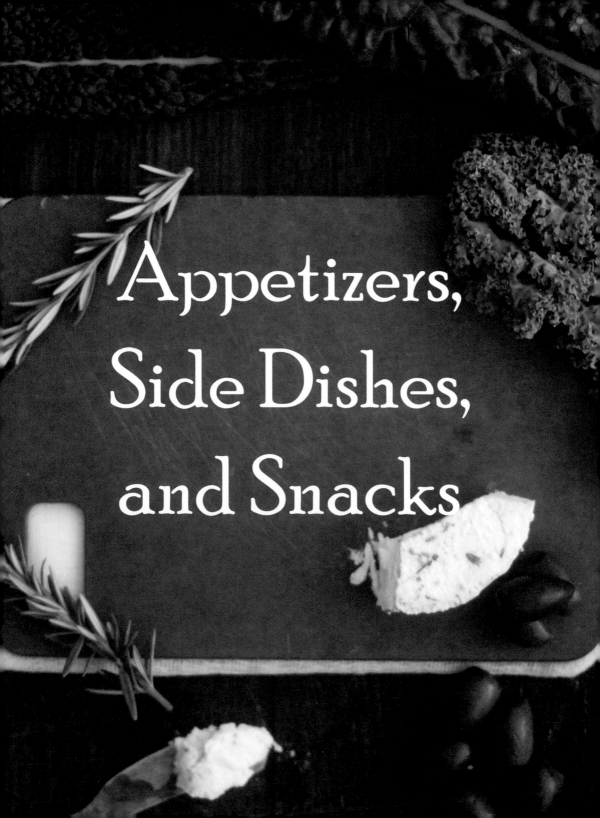

Appetizers, Side Dishes, and Snacks

Balsamic Roasted Vegetables with Beet Pesto Quinoa

Serves 8.

INSTRUCTIONS:

1. Preheat the oven to 375 degrees F. Add all vegetables except for the kale to a casserole dish.

2. In a small bowl, whisk together the oil, vinegar, garlic powder, cumin, sage, and salt. Pour this mixture over the vegetables. Mix the oil/vinegar mixture into the vegetables until everything is coated. Bake in the oven for 50 to 60 minutes, or until vegetables have browned and are cooked all the way through (test the sweet potato and beet to make sure they are cooked all the way). Stir the vegetables every 20 minutes.

3. When the vegetables are 20 minutes away from being finished, add the chopped kale leaves and mix them in with the vegetables, pushing them underneath the vegetables as much as possible. Continue roasting the remaining 20 minutes.

4. While the vegetables are roasting, you can prepare your quinoa. Rinse quinoa until the water that drains off of it is clear. Add the rinsed quinoa and 4 cups of water to a pot and bring to a full boil. Reduce the heat to a simmer, cover the pot, and cook quinoa about 15 to 20 minutes, or until all liquid is absorbed.

5. Remove quinoa from the heat and immediately stir in the Roasted Beet, Walnut, and Kale Pesto until the quinoa is well coated in the pesto. Serve quinoa with roasted vegetables on top.

INGREDIENTS:

For the Roasted Vegetables:

1 yellow onion, sliced

1 small sweet potato, chopped into ½" pieces (about 2 cups worth)

3 small golden beets, peeled and chopped into ½" pieces (about 2 cups worth)

2 cups green beans, chopped into 1½" pieces

1 head cauliflower, chopped into florets (about 4 cups)

2 tablespoons grapeseed or olive oil

2 tablespoons balsamic vinegar

1 teaspoon garlic powder

1 teaspoon ground cumin

1 teaspoon ground sage

1 teaspoon kosher salt, or to taste

6 cups tightly packed green curly kale leaves

For the Red Quinoa:

2 cups red quinoa, rinsed

⅓ cup Roasted Beet, Walnut, and Kale Pesto (pg. 193)

Vegan "Cheesy" Kale Chips

Serves 2.

INSTRUCTIONS:

1. Preheat oven to 350 degrees F.
2. In a bowl, mix all ingredients together except for the kale. Make sure the mixture is well combined.
3. Tear the kale leaves off the stems and save the stems for smoothies or other cooking. Rip the leaves in large hunks.
4. Massage the nutritional yeast mixture into each kale leaf. Avoid putting too much of the mixture on each leaf, because they can end up soggy instead of crispy.
5. Spread the kale leaves on a well-oiled baking sheet and bake for 15 to 17 minutes, until leaves are crispy. Be sure to keep an eye on the kale chips because they burn easily.

INGREDIENTS:

1 head green kale, stems removed

1 lemon, juiced (about 2 tablespoons lemon juice)

1 tablespoon tahini*

3 tablespoons grapeseed or olive oil

¼ cup + 2 tablespoons nutritional yeast

½ teaspoon garlic powder

¼ teaspoon chili powder

¼ teaspoon coarse sea salt, or to taste

*You can replace the tahini with an additional tablespoon of oil

Warning: Vegan Cheesy Kale Chips may illicit feelings of exuberance and result in addiction to kale. Kale chips are a nutritious and tasty snack to satisfy your craving for salty, crunchy potato chips. Rubbing a mixture made of nutritional yeast, spices, and oil into kale leaves mimics the flavor of cheese. Roasting kale in this mixture results in crispy chips that have a nacho cheese flavor.

Cheesy Mashed Yams

INSTRUCTIONS:

1. Bring a pot of water to a full boil. Chop the yams into large chunks and carefully place them in the boiling water (or use a steamer). Cook for 20 minutes or until yams are soft when poked with a fork. Strain the potatoes and set them aside.

2. Add 1 tablespoon of oil to a sauté pan and heat to medium. Add the chopped onion and sauté until onion begins to turn translucent. Add the garlic and sauté until onion begins to turn brown, about 15 to 20 minutes.

3. Add the onions/garlic to a blender or food processor (or a large pot for mashing by hand), along with all of the ingredients except for the kale. Blend (or mash) until smooth or desired chunkiness has been achieved.

4. Add another tablespoon of oil to the pan that you were using to sauté the onions and place it back on medium heat. Add the chopped kale leaves and stir to coat them in oil. Place a cover on top of the pan to allow the leaves to steam and soften, about 2 to 3 minutes.

5. Pour the mashed potatoes into a large serving dish and mix in the kale leaves. Stir well to combine.

6. Serve with chopped green onion and additional cheese, if desired.

INGREDIENTS:

2 large jewel yams (5 cups worth when pureed)

2 tablespoons grapeseed or olive oil, divided

1 yellow onion, chopped

4 cloves garlic, minced

1 ½ cups parmesan cheese, grated

½ teaspoon kosher salt, or to taste

3 tablespoons green onion, chopped, plus more for serving

½ cup unsweetened almond milk*

2 cups tightly packed green kale leaves, chopped

*You can replace the almond milk with buttermilk or regular milk.

Buttery, Crispy, Sautéed Kale Crostini with Beet and Kale Pesto

Makes 10 crostinis.

INSTRUCTIONS:

1. Add the butter and kale leaves to a large skillet and heat to medium-high. Cover the skillet and cook, stirring every minute or so until the kale leaves are softened but crispy, about 3 to 5 minutes. Set aside.
2. Put your oven on the high broil setting.
3. Lay the slices of bread on a baking sheet and broil for about 1 minute. Remove from the oven and lay one slice of mozzarella cheese on each slice of bread.
4. Place baking sheet back in the oven and continue to broil until mozzarella cheese is melted and bread is toasted.
5. Spread desired amount of Roasted Beet, Walnut, and Kale Pesto over the cheesy toasted bread. Top with buttery, crispy, sautéed kale and roasted garlic cloves.

INGREDIENTS:

8 cups tightly packed green curly kale leaves

2 tablespoons salted butter

2 bulbs garlic, roasted

10 slices low-moisture mozzarella cheese

10 slices rustic bread

Roasted Beet, Walnut, and Kale Pesto (pg. 193)

Typically when sautéing kale, one would leave the temperature low and sauté the leaves just until wilted. As an alternative, when you sauté kale in butter at a higher temperature, it becomes crispy, as opposed to mushy. This makes for a great texture and adds character to this delicious appetizer. Between the kale, garlic, and beet pesto, this dish is full of health benefits.

Garlic and Ginger Sautéed Kale

Serves 2.

INSTRUCTIONS:

1. Heat oil in a medium-sized skillet. Add the garlic and ginger and sauté until fragrant, about 1 minute.
2. Add the chopped kale leaves and sauté until softened and wilted, stirring constantly, about 3 to 5 minutes. Serve with fresh lemon slices as a side dish to any meal.

INGREDIENTS:

1 tablespoon olive oil

1 head dino kale, stems removed, leaves chopped

6 cloves garlic, minced

2 teaspoons ginger, peeled and grated

½ teaspoon kosher salt

One of the easiest ways of preparing kale is sautéing it. Exposing kale leaves to heat allows them to soften, so that they are not so tough, bitter, and fibrous. Simply adding salt and pepper makes for a healthful and tasty side dish, although my favorite way of preparing sautéed kale is with garlic and ginger. Also try adding your favorite spices, such as cumin, cayenne, paprika, etc.

Cheddar Kale Skillet Cornbread

INSTRUCTIONS:

1. Preheat the oven to 400 degrees F, and oil a 10" cast iron skillet.
2. In a small mixing bowl, stir together the cornmeal, oat flour, salt, baking powder, baking soda, and onion powder.
3. In a separate bowl, whisk together the milk, eggs, and butter. Add the grated cheese and kale leaves and stir until well incorporated.
4. Pour the dry mixture into the wet and stir until combined.
5. Pour the cornbread batter into the oiled skillet and smooth it with a spatula to evenly distribute it.
6. Bake in the oven for 20 to 22 minutes, or until edges are slightly browned and cornbread is cooked through.

INGREDIENTS:

1 cup finely ground cornmeal

1 cup oat flour

¼ teaspoon salt

1 teaspoon baking powder

¼ teaspoon baking soda

1 teaspoon onion powder

1 cup almond milk or
    buttermilk

2 eggs

½ cup butter, melted

¾ cup cheddar cheese, grated

2 cups kale, leaves chopped

Roasted Fingerling Potato Salad

Serves 4 to 6.

INSTRUCTIONS:

1. Preheat the oven to 425 degrees F.
2. Spread fingerling potatoes on a baking sheet or in a casserole dish and drizzle them with olive oil. Use your hands to coat all of the potatoes in oil.
3. Wrap the bulb of garlic in aluminum foil and place it on the baking sheet/casserole dish with the potatoes. Roast in the oven for 20 to 25 minutes, or until potatoes are soft when poked with a fork. Remove potatoes and garlic from the oven and allow them to cool.
4. Once cool enough to handle, peel the potato skins off and chop the potatoes into ¼" to ½" sized pieces.
5. Unwrap the garlic from the foil and peel the skins off all of the cloves. Roughly chop the garlic cloves. Add the potatoes, garlic, and green onion to a large serving bowl.
6. In a small bowl, whisk together the mayonnaise, yogurt, lemon juice, lemon zest, mustard, and salt. Pour this mixture over the potatoes and mix it in until everything is coated.
7. Sauté the kale leaves over medium heat in a small amount of oil, until leaves are softened, about 3 minutes. Allow the kale to cool, then mix them in with the potato salad. Allow salad to cool in the refrigerator for a couple of hours before serving.

INGREDIENTS:

28 ounces fingerling potatoes, roasted

2 tablespoons olive oil

1 bulb garlic, roasted

2 stalks green onion, chopped

2 tablespoons mayonnaise

2 tablespoons plain yogurt

1 tablespoon fresh lemon juice

Zest of 1 lemon

2 teaspoons whole grain mustard

½ teaspoon salt, or to taste

2 cups packed curly green kale leaves, chopped and sautéed

Southwest Stuffed Bell Peppers

Serves 10.

INSTRUCTIONS:

1. Bring 2 cups of water to a boil and add in the brown rice. Return to a full boil, add the chili powder and salt, then immediately lower the heat and simmer for 35 to 40 minutes, or until the rice has absorbed all of the water.

2. Heat the oil in a large sauté pan over medium heat. Add the red onion and sauté 5 minutes, until it begins turning translucent. Add the garlic and sauté an additional minute. Add the kale leaves and stir, allowing the leaves to get coated with oil. Cook until leaves are softened, about 2 minutes. Remove from heat and set aside.

3. Preheat the oven to 425 degrees F.

4. Once the rice is ready, add the rice, corn kernels, and black beans to the pan with the onion and kale. Mix everything together.

5. Cut the bell peppers in half lengthwise and remove the insides and the stems.

6. Place the bell peppers on a baking sheet, cut-side up. Spoon the rice mixture into the bell peppers.

7. Bake peppers in the oven for 12 minutes.

8. Remove the peppers from the oven, add grated cheese on top, and put them back in the oven for 8 to 10 minutes, until cheese is melted and golden.

INGREDIENTS:

1 cup brown rice

2 teaspoons chili powder

½ teaspoon salt, or to taste

1 tablespoon olive oil

½ cup red onion, finely chopped

4 cloves garlic, minced

4 cups tightly packed kale leaves, chopped

1 cup fresh corn kernels, cooked

1 cup black beans, rinsed and drained

5 bell peppers (color of choice), halved lengthwise, insides and stems removed

Shredded jack cheese

Spanish Cauliflower "Rice"

Serves 4.

INSTRUCTIONS:

1. Remove the green stems from the cauliflower and chop the head in half. Using a box grater, grate the whole head of cauliflower (one half at a time).
2. In a large skillet, heat the oil to medium-high and sauté the onion until fragrant and slightly softened, about 3 minutes.
3. Add the grated cauliflower, garlic, and jalapeño to the skillet and stir consistently until the cauliflower begins to cook down and turn brown, about 5 to 8 minutes.
4. Reduce the heat to medium, add the kale leaves and stir them into the cauliflower rice. Cover the skillet, allowing the kale leaves to soften about 2 minutes.
5. Add the diced tomatoes, salt, and chili powder, and stir them into the "rice."
6. Continue cooking another 2 to 3 minutes to allow some of the moisture to burn off, stirring consistently.
7. Serve the Spanish Cauliflower Rice alongside your favorite meal!

INGREDIENTS:

2 tablespoons olive oil

1 yellow onion, chopped

1 head cauliflower, grated (stems removed)

6 cloves garlic, minced

1 jalapeño, seeded and finely chopped

2 cups tightly packed green kale leaves

1 14.5-ounce can diced tomatoes (unsalted)

1 teaspoon salt, or to taste

1½ tablespoons chili powder

Cauliflower rice is a great alternative to regular rice. It has a similar texture, can be flavored just like regular rice, and can be applied to any dish or meal to take the place of any grain. This recipe mimics one of my favorite rice dishes, Spanish-style rice. Adding kale into the mix makes the already nutritious dish even more nutrientdense!

Superfood Stuffed Acorn Squash

Serves 6.

INSTRUCTIONS:

To Prepare the Roasted Acorn Squash and Beets:

1. Preheat the oven to 375 degrees F.
2. Cut the tip and tail off of each acorn squash, and then lengthwise. Scoop the seeds and innards out of each half.
3. Place the acorn squash cut-side up on a baking sheet. Drizzle each half with about a tablespoon of olive oil, so that all of the flesh is lightly coated. Drizzle each half with about a tablespoon (or two) of honey. Sprinkle kosher salt and cinnamon over the squash.
4. Chop each beet into ½" cubes and place on a long sheet of foil. Wrap the chopped beets in the foil, creating a packet, and place the foil packet on the baking sheet along with the acorn squash.
5. Roast the squash and the beets in the oven for 45 to 50 minutes, or until the squash is very tender when poked with a fork and the beets are cooked through.

Continued on next page . . .

INGREDIENTS:

3 acorn squash, halved

6 tablespoons olive oil

6 tablespoons honey

Kosher salt

Cinnamon

2 medium-sized beets

For the Quinoa Stuffing:

1½ cups uncooked quinoa

Zest of 1 orange

½ cup fresh orange juice (1 navel orange, juiced)

3 tablespoons olive oil

½ teaspoon cinnamon

1 teaspoon kosher salt

6 cups dino kale leaves, thinly sliced

1 pear, chopped

¾ cup dried cranberries

½ cup pecans, chopped

2 ounces goat chevre, crumbled

To Prepare the Quinoa stuffing:

1. Rinse the quinoa well and soak it in a large pot for about 10 minutes.
2. Drain the quinoa and add 1½ cups of water to the pot. Bring the quinoa to a full boil, then reduce the heat to medium–low, cover the pot, and allow the quinoa to simmer until all of the water is absorbed, about 15 minutes.
3. As soon as the quinoa is finished cooking, fluff it with a fork and stir in the chopped kale leaves so that the steam helps the leaves soften. Cover the pot and allow it to sit for about 5 minutes.
4. In a small bowl, whisk together the orange zest, orange juice, olive oil, cinnamon, and salt. Pour the orange dressing over the quinoa and kale and mix it together.
5. Add the chopped pear, dried cranberries, pecans, goat cheese, and roasted beets to the pot and mix everything together well.
6. Scoop desired amount of quinoa stuffing into each acorn squash and serve!

OPTIONAL:

If desired, grate gruyere cheese over each stuffed acorn squash, and place them in the oven under the broil setting until the cheese is melted and slightly browned, about 2 minutes.

Packed with fall harvest goodies, including pears, pecans, dried cranberries, and beets, and tossed with quinoa and an orange-cinnamon dressing, this dish is just as delicious as it is nutritious. It includes protein from the quinoa and pecans, as well as numerous vitamins and minerals from all of the vegetables. Skip the acorn squash and turn this recipe into a delicious fall quinoa salad if desired!

Turkey Sliders with Caramelized Onions, Sautéed Kale, and Blue Cheese

Makes 6 sliders.

INSTRUCTIONS:

1. Add all ingredients for the burger patties to a mixing bowl. Use your hands to mix everything together well. In a large skillet, heat enough oil to coat the surface.

2. Form small burger patties out of the meat and place onto the hot skillet. Allow the patties to cook until browned and sides of the patties begin to firm up, about 3 to 5 minutes.

3. Flip and cook on the other side another 3 to 5 minutes. Poke the top of the burgers—if the meat feels firm and the juice that seeps out is clear, the burgers are finished. If the meat feels mushy and the juice is pink, allow the patties to continue to cook.

4. To prepare the slider toppings, heat the oil in a large skillet. Add the sliced onions and sauté, stirring every few minutes until onions are beginning to caramelize, about 30 minutes.

5. Add the mushrooms and cook until mushrooms have cooked down and have browned, about another 10 minutes.

6. Add the chopped kale leaves and cover the sauté pan. Allow the leaves to steam until they have softened and wilted, about 3 minutes.

7. Toast the slider buns. Add slider patties, desired amount of veggies, chimichurri sauce, and blue cheese crumbles to the buns. Enjoy your delicious sliders!

INGREDIENTS:

For the Slider Meat:

1 pound ground turkey meat

1 tablespoon fresh oregano leaves, finely chopped

1 tablespoon chimichurri sauce (from pg. 183) or olive oil

¼ teaspoon salt

1 teaspoon garlic powder

For the Burger Toppings:

2 tablespoons grapeseed or olive oil

1 large yellow onion, sliced

8 baby portobello mushrooms, chopped

6 cups tightly packed kale leaves, chopped

Chimichurri sauce (pg. 183)

Blue cheese crumbles

6 slider buns, toasted

Zesty Kale Slaw

Serves 8.

INSTRUCTIONS:

1. Cut a red cabbage in half, remove and discard the core, and thinly slice both halves.
2. Peel a carrot and chop it into thin, small matchsticks.
3. Remove the leaves of dino kale from the stems (saving the stems for cooking or smoothies) and thinly slice the leaves.
4. Using the fine side of a box grater, finely grate fresh, peeled ginger.
5. In a small bowl, whisk together the olive oil, lime zest, lime juice, grated ginger, garlic, and salt.
6. Add the vegetables to a large mixing bowl and pour the dressing on top.
7. Mix well until everything is coated in the dressing.
8. Serve on barbecue or deli sandwiches, on tacos, or as a side dish!

Note: Also try this recipe with beets instead of cabbage! Peel and chop beets into sixths, place in a food processor, and pulse until shredded. You can also replace the lime zest and juice with orange zest and juice.

INGREDIENTS:

1 small head red cabbage
   (about 7 cups thinly sliced)
1 large carrot
1 head dino kale
1 tablespoon olive oil
Zest of 1 lime
¼ cup fresh lime juice
1 tablespoon ginger, peeled
   and finely grated
1 clove garlic, minced
¼ to ½ teaspoon salt, or to
   taste

Zucchini, Kale, and Leek Fritters with Yogurt Dipping Sauce

Makes 8 fritters.

INSTRUCTIONS:

1. Prepare the yogurt sauce. Combine all ingredients in a bowl and stir to mix. Place in refrigerator to keep cool.
2. Preheat the oven to 400 degrees F.
3. Wrap the garlic cloves (with skin on) in tinfoil and roast for 20 minutes. Remove from the oven and allow garlic to cool. When cool enough to handle, remove garlic skin and finely chop.
4. Rinse the zucchini and pat dry. Chop the zucchini into quarters and pulse 8 to 10 times in a food processor or until shredded but not mushy.
5. Put the zucchini shreds into a colander with a bowl underneath. Sprinkle salt over the shreds, toss with your hands, and place the colander and bowl in the refrigerator for at least 2 hours to allow the moisture to seep out. Squeeze any remaining moisture out with your hands.
6. Wash and chop the leek into quarters and place in the food processor. Pulse 8 to 10 times, or until leek is finely chopped.
7. Preheat oven to 375 degrees F. and prepare a lightly oiled baking sheet or line a baking sheet with parchment paper.
8. Transfer the shredded zucchini, leek, and chopped kale to a mixing bowl.

INGREDIENTS:

For the Fritters:

1 medium-sized leek (about 2 cups), chopped

1 large zucchini squash (about 2 cups)

2 cups green kale leaves, finely chopped

1 teaspoon kosher salt

½ teaspoon black pepper

3 cloves garlic, roasted and chopped

2 eggs, lightly beaten

1 ¼ cup shredded parmesan cheese, separated

½ cup panko breadcrumbs

For the Dipping Sauce:

½ cup plain yogurt

1 tablespoon green onion, finely chopped

Zest of 1 lemon

1 clove garlic, minced

Pinch of salt

Continued on next page . . .

9. In a small bowl, lightly beat two eggs and pour over the vegetables. Add ¾ cup of the grated parmesan along with the salt, pepper, and chopped roasted garlic. Stir well to incorporate.

10. On a plate, mix together ½ cup of the grated parmesan cheese and the bread crumbs.

11. Form patties out of the vegetable mixture, coat them in the bread crumb mixture, and place on a well-oiled or parchment–lined baking sheet.

12. Bake for 25 to 30 minutes, until the bottoms of the fritters crisp up, then remove from oven. Carefully flip the fritters using a spatula and bake another 8 to 10 minutes until edges are crispy and the fritters feel dry when poked.

13. Serve fritters with yogurt dipping sauce!

Notes:

1. If you don't have a food processor, shred the zucchini and finely chop the leek.

2. If your fritter patties seem overly wet, you can add additional breadcrumbs to the patty mixture in order to make the mixture easier to work with.

These oven-baked fritters make a great appetizer and are a healthier alternative to the fried version. Already packed with flavor, these fritters are made even better when served with a yogurt dipping sauce to go with them. Make these for a healthy snack, as a side dish, or as an appetizer.

Salads

Beet and Kale Slaw Salad with Tahini-Orange Dressing

Serves 6.

INSTRUCTIONS:

1. Bring a full pot of water to a boil. Add the beets and carrots and return to a boil.
2. Allow the vegetables to cook until somewhat soft when poked, but still firm. The carrots will only need about 8 minutes, but medium–sized beets should require 25.
3. Strain the vegetables and allow them to cool. When cool enough to handle, grate the veggies using a box grater and add to a large bowl.
4. Wash the kale well, but don't pat it dry. Thinly slice all of the leaves, discarding the stems (or save for later for smoothies). Place the sliced leaves in a skillet. Heat the skillet, covered, over medium heat. Cook just until wilted, about 2 minutes, stirring to allow all of the leaves to soften. Immediately remove from the heat and add them to the bowl with the beets and carrots.
5. In a small bowl, whisk together all of the ingredients for the dressing. Pour the dressing over the veggies and toss well.
6. Serve salad with large hunks of avocado, a dollop of coconut milk, and sesame seeds on top.

Note: You can keep this salad raw by not boiling the vegetables and using a food processor to process them.

INGREDIENTS:

For the Salad:

3 medium-sized beets

4 large carrots

Ripe avocado, for serving

1 head dino kale, thinly sliced

1 cup unsweetened shredded coconut

For the Tahini-Orange Dressing:

4 tablespoons tahini

½ cup orange juice

Zest of 1 orange

1 tablespoon fresh ginger, peeled and finely grated

1 teaspoon kosher salt

½ teaspoon cinnamon

1 teaspoon ground cumin

½ teaspoon ground turmeric

Fall Harvest Kale Salad with Cinnamon-Orange Dressing

Serves 4.

INSTRUCTIONS:

1. Preheat the oven to 400 degrees F.
2. Chop the top and bottom off the acorn squash, then cut it in half lengthwise (from tip to tail).
3. Chop the acorn squash into ½" slices, then scoop the seeds out of the slices.
4. Place the slices of acorn squash on a baking sheet and coat the pieces well with oil on both sides.
5. Roast in the oven for 50 minutes, or until squash is crispy on the outside and soft in the middle.
6. Remove from the oven and allow squash to cool. Once cool enough to handle, peel the outer skin off of the squash flesh and discard the skin (note: you can also serve the salad with the skin on— they are edible and very nutritious).
7. In a small bowl, whisk together the salad dressing ingredients.
8. Add all salad ingredients to a large salad bowl.
9. Toss in desired amount of dressing and serve.

INGREDIENTS:

For the Salad:

1 acorn squash, sliced

½ bosc pear, sliced

⅓ cup pecans, roasted

5 ounces baby kale

For the Dressing:

1 teaspoon orange zest

⅓ cup fresh orange juice

1 tablespoon balsamic vinegar

1 tablespoon maple syrup

3 tablespoons olive oil

¼ teaspoon ground cinnamon

⅛ teaspoon kosher salt

Green Quinoa Salad with Asparagus, Avocado, and Kale Pesto

INSTRUCTIONS:

1. Using a fine strainer, rinse the quinoa very well with water until the water that comes off of it is clear, not cloudy.

2. Put the quinoa in a saucepan and soak it for 10 minutes. Drain the water. Add 2 cups of water to the saucepan with the quinoa and bring it to a boil on the stovetop. Reduce heat and simmer for 15 to 20 minutes, or until quinoa absorbs all of the moisture. Remove from heat, fluff quinoa with a fork, and set aside.

3. In a sauté pan, heat about a tablespoon of oil to medium-high. Add the chopped asparagus and sauté until color turns bright green and asparagus begins to soften, about 3 to 5 minutes.

4. Add the chopped kale and stir. Cover the sauté pan and allow kale to wilt, about 1 to 2 minutes. Add the kale pesto to the cooked quinoa and stir until combined. Pour the pesto quinoa into the sauté pan with the asparagus and kale.

5. Add lemon zest, salt, and roasted walnuts and stir together. Pour the quinoa salad into a large serving dish and garnish with avocado and feta cheese.

INGREDIENTS:

1 cup quinoa

2 cups water

1 tablespoon olive oil

2 cups asparagus, chopped

3 cups tightly packed kale leaves, roughly chopped

Zest of 1 lemon

½ teaspoon salt, or to taste

¼ cup + 1 tablespoon Kale and Pistachio Pesto (pg. 187) (or pesto sauce of choice)

½ cup walnuts, roasted

1 ripe avocado, diced

¼ cup feta cheese, crumbled

Notes:

1. You can gently fold the avocado and feta cheese into the quinoa salad prior to serving or serve on top.

2. This salad is delicious both warm and cold!

Grilled Kale, Peach, and Corn Salad with Basil Honey Balsamic Vinaigrette

Serves 4 to 6.

INSTRUCTIONS:

To Prepare the Dressing:

Add all dressing ingredients to a small bowl and whisk together until well combined. Set aside (or refrigerate).

To Prepare the Grilled Kale Salad:

1. Heat your grill to medium-high or high.
2. Lightly coat each of the kale leaves (including stems) in high-temperature oil of choice.
3. Lightly coat the cut-side of the peaches with oil. If desired, sprinkle peaches with salt, cinnamon, and/or brown sugar. Place peaches on the grill and cook until softened, golden brown, and juices are seeping out.
4. Add kale leaves to the grill and cook on each side about 30 seconds to 1 minute, just until kale begins to brown and slightly soften.
5. Place whole kale leaves and halved peaches on a platter. Sprinkle with feta cheese, salt, and pepper. Drizzle the dressing and serve.

INGREDIENTS:

For the Dressing:

1 tablespoon balsamic vinegar

1 tablespoon olive oil

1 teaspoon stone-ground mustard

1 teaspoon honey

1 teaspoon fresh basil leaves, finely chopped (about 4 basil leaves)

Salt and pepper to taste

For the Salad:

1 ear corn, grilled, shucked, and kernels removed

3 ripe (but firm) peaches, halved

1 to 2 tablespoons grapeseed or coconut oil (or high-temperature cooking oil of choice)

1 head dino kale

Feta cheese

Salt and pepper to taste

Kale and Chickpea Salad with Ginger-Tahini Dressing

Serves 4.

INSTRUCTIONS:

1. Bring 2 cups of water to a boil. Add brown rice and return to a boil. Reduce heat and simmer for 35 to 40 minutes, until all water is absorbed.
2. Once rice is finished cooking, add nutritional yeast and stir well to make "cheesy" vegan rice.
3. In a small bowl, whisk together the dressing ingredients and set aside (the dressing will be a thick paste). Add the chopped kale leaves, onion, chickpeas, and avocado to a large salad bowl.
4. Toss the salad with the ginger–tahini dressing. Serve salad with brown rice.

INGREDIENTS:

For the Salad:

1 cup uncooked brown rice

2 cups water

3 tablespoons nutritional yeast

6 cups tightly packed dino kale leaves, sliced into thin strips

½ cup red onion, thinly sliced

1 cup chickpeas, drained and rinsed

1 avocado, pitted and diced

For the Ginger-Tahini Dressing:

3 tablespoons tahini

3 tablespoons white vinegar

1 tablespoon peeled and grated fresh ginger

Pinch of salt

Massaged Kale Salad with Rosemary Candied Walnuts and Creamy Blueberry Vinaigrette

Serves 4 to 6.

INGREDIENTS:

For the Creamy Blueberry Vinaigrette:

⅓ cup grapeseed oil

3 tablespoons white vinegar

1½ cups fresh blueberries (makes about half a cup of syrup)

2 to 3 tablespoons honey

⅓ cup plain yogurt

½ teaspoon salt

For the Rosemary Candied Walnuts:

1 cup walnut halves

1 teaspoon grapeseed or olive oil

1 tablespoon honey

1 teaspoon fresh or dried rosemary

Pinch of salt

Dash of cinnamon

Dash of ground ginger

For the Massaged Kale Salad:

1 head kale, stems removed and discarded, leaves chopped

Juice of half a lemon (about a tablespoon)

¼ red onion, thinly sliced

1 pint blueberries

1 cup rosemary candied walnuts (recipe below)

½ cup goat cheese, crumbled

Blueberry vinaigrette (recipe below)

Continued on next page . . .

INSTRUCTIONS:

To Prepare the Creamy Blueberry Vinaigrette:

1. In a covered saucepan, heat the blueberries and honey over medium heat until blueberry juices are seeping out and bubbly.
2. Mash blueberries with a fork to help get juices out and cook an additional 5 minutes, but don't allow the mixture to boil over. Remove from heat and strain blueberry syrup using a fine wire strainer. Discard the blueberry pulp and place blueberry syrup in the refrigerator to cool.
3. Once cool, combine blueberry syrup with all other ingredients for the vinaigrette and mix vigorously with a whisk until smooth and creamy (or place everything in a blender and blend until smooth and creamy). Place in the refrigerator until ready to use.

To Prepare the Salad:

Place the chopped kale leaves in a salad bowl and drizzle the lemon juice over the leaves. Massage leaves with your hands about 2 minutes and let sit about 10 minutes in order to allow leaves to soften. Add all other salad ingredients to salad bowl and set aside.

To Prepare the Rosemary Candied Walnuts:

1. Using a small skillet, heat the grapeseed oil, honey, and rosemary over medium–low heat. Add the walnuts and stir to coat.
2. Sprinkle a touch of cinnamon, ground ginger, and salt over the walnuts and allow nuts to continue to toast another 3 to 5 minutes, stirring consistently.
3. Don't allow nuts to sit without stirring because the honey will burn onto the nuts quickly when unattended. The nuts are ready when they are soft yet toasty, warm all the way through, and have a nice sweet glaze on the outside.
4. Sprinkle the walnuts over the salad and drizzle blueberry vinaigrette over everything to taste. Toss with your hands or salad tongs to ensure everything is evenly coated. Enjoy!

Note: Use leftover Creamy Blueberry Vinaigrette for other salads! Store in a sealed container in the refrigerator for up to 1 week and stir before using.

Mediterranean Quinoa and Kale Salad

Serves 12.

INSTRUCTIONS:

1. Rinse the quinoa until the water that runs off of it is clear. Soak the quinoa for about 10 minutes in a large saucepan. Drain the water, add 3 ¾ cups of water to the saucepan, and bring to a full boil.

2. Reduce the heat to medium–low, cover the saucepan, and simmer for 15 to 20 minutes, or until all of the water is absorbed.

3. A few minutes before the quinoa is finished cooking, add the chopped kale, allowing the leaves to sit on top of the quinoa to steam (do not mix the kale into the quinoa until the quinoa is finished cooking all the way).

4. Remove the cover, fluff quinoa with a fork, stir in the steamed kale leaves, and add the mixture to a large serving bowl.

5. In a small bowl, whisk together the vinegar, olive oil, zest, lemon juice, and salt. Pour this dressing over the quinoa and mix well.

6. Add the remaining ingredients to the bowl with the quinoa and stir together. Serve with additional feta cheese on top.

INGREDIENTS:

2 cups uncooked quinoa, rinsed and drained

⅓ cup red wine vinegar

⅓ cup olive oil

Zest of 1 lemon

2 lemons, juiced

1 teaspoon salt

1½ cups sun-dried tomatoes, julienne cut*

1½ cups pitted kalamata olives, chopped into thirds

4 cups tightly packed kale leaves, roughly chopped

½ cup feta cheese, crumbled, plus more for serving

This classic Mediterranean-style quinoa salad is perfect to make for large gatherings. It is chock full of flavors and can be served alongside a wide variety of dishes. With nutty, creamy, tangy, zesty flavors, this salad is a wonderful alternative to pasta salads!

Raw Broccoli and Kale Salad

INSTRUCTIONS:

1. Wash kale leaves and pat them dry. Remove the stems (save stems for a smoothie or other cooking), chop the kale leaves into small strips, and place in a serving bowl. Drizzle the lemon juice over the kale leaves and use your hands to massage the leaves until dark green and softened. Allow the leaves to sit 10 minutes.

2. Chop the broccoli into small florets and add to the serving bowl along with the grapes, red onion, cranberries, and sunflower seeds.

3. In a small bowl, mix together the yogurt, honey, and salt. Pour all of this mixture over the salad and toss well to ensure everything is coated.

4. Taste the salad and add additional salt to taste. Serve with your favorite entree!

INGREDIENTS:

4 cups tightly packed curly green kale leaves, chopped

½ lemon, juiced (about 1½ tablespoons lemon juice)

2 small crowns broccoli, chopped into small florets (about 5 cups)

1½ cups seedless red grapes, halved

1 cup red onion, thinly sliced

¾ cup dried cranberries

½ cup sunflower seeds

1 cup plain yogurt

1 tablespoon honey

½ teaspoon kosher salt

Broccoli salad, or as some affectionately refer to as "family reunion salad," is an easy, delicious, and healthful salad to serve at your family barbecue or get-together. Instead of using mayonnaise with sugar for the dressing, I love using plain yogurt and honey, which keeps the salad light, natural, and healthful.

Roasted Beet and Fig Massaged Kale Salad with Blackberry Vinaigrette

Serves 4.

INSTRUCTIONS:

To Prepare the Blackberry Vinaigrette:

1. Heat the balsamic vinegar and berries in a saucepan over medium heat, covered. Bring to a full boil.
2. Remove cover and smash blackberries with a fork, allowing the mixture to continue to boil. Reduce the liquid by ⅓. Add the honey and stir to incorporate.
3. Use a fine strainer to strain out the blackberry pulp and push on the pulp with a spoon to release as much of the juices as possible.
4. Pour the blackberry balsamic vinegar into a jar and put it in the refrigerator to cool.

Continued on next page . . .

INGREDIENTS:

For the Salad:

1 large or 2 small red beets

6 cups tightly packed green or Russian kale leaves, chopped

6 figs, quartered

¼ cup walnuts

¼ cup blue cheese, crumbled

2 lemons, juiced

For the Blackberry Vinaigrette:

¾ cup fresh ripe blackberries

½ cup balsamic vinegar

2 teaspoons honey

¼ cup grapeseed or olive oil

Have you ever infused your own balsamic vinegar to give it a rich, sweet, delicious flavor? If no, scamper off to the kitchen, and do so stat! The homemade blackberry vinaigrette on this salad really ties the whole thing together like a well-matched belt or handbag . . . or something like that.

To Prepare the Roasted Beet and Fig Salad:

1. Preheat oven to 400 degrees F.
2. Scrub the beet and chop off the greens (stems). You can discard the beet greens or use them in another recipe.
3. Dice the beet into ¼" to ½" cubes. Place the chopped beet on a sheet of aluminum foil. Fold the edges of the foil over on top of each other, creating a package of beet.
4. Put the beet package on a cookie sheet and roast in the oven for 50 minutes or until beets are soft when poked with a fork. Remove from the oven and set aside to cool.
5. 15 minutes before the beets are finished roasting, quarter the figs and place them on a parchment-lined cookie sheet. Roast them for 10 to 12 minutes, until their juices begin seeping out. Remove from oven and set aside.
6. While the beets and figs are roasting, wash the kale leaves, remove the stems, and chop the leaves.
7. Place the chopped leaves into a large salad bowl and drizzle the juice from 2 lemons over the leaves. Using your hands, massage the lemon juice into the leaves. Allow the leaves to sit at least 10 minutes so the lemon juice softens the leaves.
8. When ready to serve the salad, add the roasted beets, figs, walnuts, and blue cheese to the salad bowl with the kale leaves.
9. Drizzle desired amount of blackberry balsamic vinaigrette over the salad and toss everything together.
10. Salad can be served lukewarm (if the beets are still warm) or cold!

Notes:

1. The blackberry vinaigrette is more "vinegar-y" than a typical vinaigrette, which is how I prefer my salald dressing. To lower the vinegar bite, simply add more oil (an additional ¼ cup).
2. You can also roast the walnuts to give them a deeper flavor and wonderful texture. Simply lay them on a cookie sheet and roast them for about 5 to 8 minutes (with the beets and figs) or until they turn slightly darker and are toasted.

Southwest Baby Kale Salad with Cumin-Ginger-Sage Dressing

INSTRUCTIONS:

To Prepare the Salad Dressing:

Add all ingredients to a blender and blend until completely combined and creamy.

To Prepare the Salad:

Add salad ingredients to a large serving bowl. Add in desired amount of Cumin Ginger Sage—Dressing and toss together so that everything is coated. Serve alongside your favorite main dish or add cooked chicken or shrimp to make this an entrée.

INGREDIENTS:

For the Salad:

5 ounces baby kale

½ cup black beans, drained and rinsed

½ cup white corn kernels

½ cup red bell pepper, chopped (about ½ a red bell pepper)

1 stalk green onion, chopped

1 ripe avocado, diced

2 hard boiled eggs, chopped

For the Cumin Ginger Sage—Dressing:

1" piece ginger, grated

5 cloves garlic, minced

8 fresh sage leaves, chopped

½ cup grapeseed or olive oil

¼ cup apple cider vinegar

¼ cup balsamic vinegar

1 tablespoon ground cumin

Thai Chicken Chopped Salad

Serves 4.

INGREDIENTS:

For the Salad:

1 boneless, skinless chicken breast,
   grilled or roasted

Chili powder and salt

5 cups Brussels sprouts, shaved*

3 cups tightly packed dino kale leaves,
   thinly sliced

1 large carrot, chopped into small
   matchsticks

1 mango, peeled, cored, and diced

¼ cup cilantro leaves, roughly chopped
   (optional)

1 tablespoon olive oil

Zest of 1 lime

¼ cup fresh lime juice

Continued on next page . . .

1 tablespoon fresh ginger, peeled and
   finely grated

1 clove garlic, minced

¼ teaspoon salt, or to taste

Thai Peanut Sauce for serving

For the Thai Peanut Sauce Dressing:

1 cup full-fat coconut milk

½ cup unsalted, unsweetened creamy
   peanut butter

1 teaspoon yellow curry powder

2 tablespoons soy sauce

1 tablespoon white vinegar

1 tablespoon fresh ginger, grated

¼ to ½ teaspoon sriracha sauce (or
   similar red chili sauce), optional

*You can replace shaved brussels sprouts with thinly
   sliced cabbage.

Don't be fooled by the long list of ingredients for this salad, or by the fact that one of those ingredients is Brussels sprouts. If you've never tried a shaved Brussels sprouts salad, I highly recommend it. This salad is a great change-up to your ordinary Thai chopped salad. The shaved Brussels and kale, combined with chicken and mango, all slathered in a delicious peanut dressing makes for an incredibly nutritious, delicious, and filling entrée salad. Jump in, Brussels sprouts naysayers, you may just acquire an addiction to this salad!

INSTRUCTIONS:

For the Thai Peanut Sauce:

Add all ingredients to a blender and blend until completely smooth. The consistency of the sauce should be thick, but if you desire a thinner consistency, simply add water.

For the Salad:

1. Preheat the oven to 350 degrees F.
2. Sprinkle the chicken breast with salt and chili powder. Place it in a lightly oiled baking dish and bake for 30 minutes or until cooked all the way through. Remove from the oven, chop the chicken, and set aside.
3. Wash the Brussels sprouts, chop off all of the hard stems, and remove the leaves that fall off easily. Thinly slice Brussels sprouts from tip-to-tail. Stop slicing once you get to the hard white core. You can either discard the core or chop it finely.
4. Place shaved Brussels in a large salad bowl. Using your hands, break apart any slices of sprouts that are stuck together (this can usually be achieved by simply tossing the shaved Brussels sprouts).
5. Wash the dino kale leaves and pat them dry. Slice them thinly and add them to the bowl with the shaved Brussels sprouts along with the chopped cilantro and diced mango.
6. In a small bowl, whisk together the olive oil, lime juice, grated ginger, garlic, and salt. Pour the dressing over the salad and toss well to be sure everything is coated. Serve salad with chopped chicken and desired amount of Thai peanut sauce on top.

Notes:

1. You will end up with far more peanut sauce than you need. You can use this to marinade chicken, add to stir-fry or satays, or use for more salads.
2. When you refrigerate the peanut sauce, it will set up because of the coconut milk and peanut butter. Before using it, simply add a small amount of water and stir until smooth.

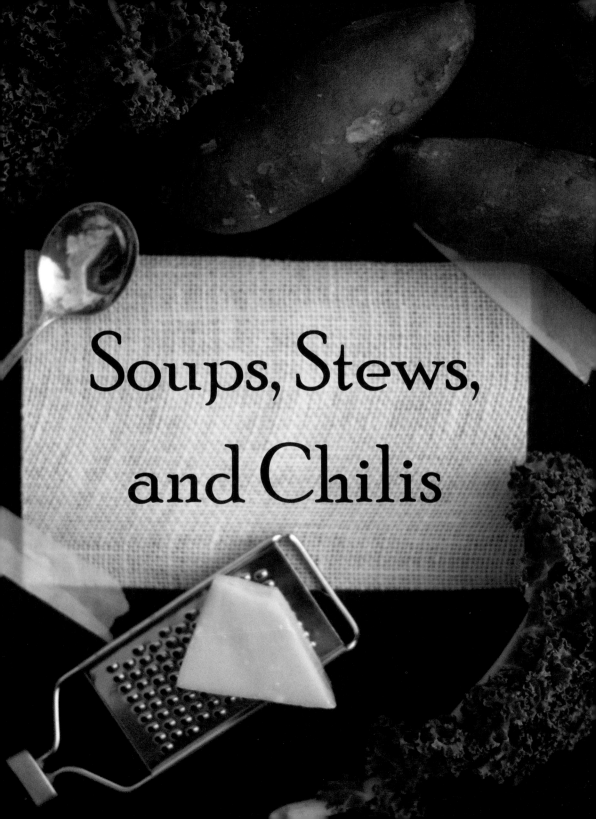

Soups, Stews, and Chilis

Butternut Squash and Kale Chili

Serves 6.

INSTRUCTIONS:

1. In a large stock pot or Dutch oven, add the oil, onion, celery, and butternut squash and heat to medium. Sauté, stirring frequently, until veggies are softened and fragrant, about 12 to 15 minutes. Add the garlic, salt, and spices and sauté another 2 minutes.

2. Add the chicken broth and diced tomatoes and bring chili to a full boil. Reduce the heat to medium-low and cover the pot. Simmer 40 to 50 minutes, or until vegetables are cooked all the way through.

3. A few minutes before you're ready to serve the chili, add the chickpeas and kale. Stir them into the chili and continue cooking until kale has softened and wilted, about 5 to 8 minutes.

4. Serve the chili with your favorite toppings and brown rice.

INGREDIENTS:

1 large red onion, chopped

1 small butternut squash, peeled and chopped (3 cups worth)

2 celery stalks, chopped

3 cloves garlic, minced

1 15-ounce can chickpeas, drained and rinsed

1 15-ounce can diced tomatoes, with liquid from can

1 cup chicken broth

2 tablespoons chili powder

2 teaspoons cumin

¼ teaspoon ground sage

¼ teaspoon cinnamon

½ teaspoon salt, or to taste

4 cups tightly packed curly kale leaves, chopped

For Serving:

Brown rice

Sour cream or plain yogurt

Your favorite chili toppings

Chilled Asparagus and Leek Soup (Vichyssoise)

Serves 4.

INSTRUCTIONS:

1. Preheat the oven to 400 degrees F.
2. Poke holes in the potato, wrap it in aluminum foil, and roast it in the oven for 1 hour, or until soft.
3. In a Dutch oven or large pot, heat the oil to medium and add the chopped leeks and asparagus. Sauté, stirring consistently until asparagus has softened but is still al dente.
4. Add the chopped kale and garlic, cover the pot, and allow the kale to soften, about 2 to 3 minutes.
5. Add the coconut milk, 1 cup of the almond milk, salt, lemon zest, and lemon juice to a blender with the sautéed greens. Blend until completely smooth. Pour the mixture back into the Dutch oven.
6. Once the potato has finished roasting, allow it to cool and then add it to a blender with the remaining almond milk. Blend until smooth.
7. Add this mixture to the Dutch oven with the blended asparagus soup and stir together until completely combined (you can also blend portions of the soup together in the blender in batches).
8. Chill in the refrigerator until completely cool and serve with yogurt and oil drizzled on top.

INGREDIENTS:

1 medium jewel yam, roasted (about 2 cups worth)*

2 tablespoons olive oil

2 medium leeks, chopped

1 bunch asparagus, stems removed, chopped

8 cloves garlic, minced

4 cups kale leaves

1 cup coconut milk (full-fat canned coconut milk recommended)

3 cups unsweetened almond milk

2 teaspoons salt

Zest of 1 lemon

2 tablespoons fresh lemon juice

Yogurt/crème fraiche and pepper for serving

*You can also use russet or red potatoes, but the jewel yam gives the soup a natural sweetness, which enhances the flavor.

Creamy Sweet Potato and Kale Soup

Serves 4.

INSTRUCTIONS:

1. Preheat the oven to 400 degrees F.
2. Using a fork, poke several holes in the sweet potato. Wrap the sweet potato in foil and roast it in the oven for 50 to 60 minutes, or until cooked through.
3. Add oil to a skillet and heat to medium. Add the onion and sauté until completely softened and browned, about 12 to 15 minutes. Add the spices and salt and sauté an additional 2 minutes.
4. Add the chopped kale leaves and cover the skillet. Allow the kale leaves to cook and soften, about 1 to 2 minutes.
5. Add the sautéed onion/kale mixture to a blender along with the roasted sweet potato, vegetable broth, and coconut milk. Blend until completely smooth. If the soup is not hot when it is finished blending, you can pour it into a saucepan and heat until desired temperature is reached.
6. Serve soup with rustic bread and enjoy!

INGREDIENTS:

1 large sweet potato, roasted

2 tablespoons grapeseed or olive oil

1 yellow onion, chopped

4 cloves garlic, minced

1 teaspoon ground cumin

1 teaspoon ground coriander

1 teaspoon ground ginger

½ teaspoon ground turmeric

Salt to taste

4 cups tightly packed green curly kale leaves, chopped

3 cups vegetable broth

1 cup coconut milk (use full-fat canned coconut milk)

Crock Pot Moroccan Lentil Stew

Serves 6 to 8.

INSTRUCTIONS:

1. Add all ingredients to a crock pot and stir well. Cook on the lowest setting for 6 to 7 hours.
2. About 30 minutes before ready to serve, add the chopped kale leaves and continue to cook until leaves are softened.
3. Once lentils are fully cooked, add ¼ to ½ of the soup to a blender and blend until smooth. Pour this mixture back into the crock pot, and stir it into the rest of the soup.
4. Serve with golden raisins and plain yogurt on top. Save leftovers for 7 to 10 days in the refrigerator. When you reheat the soup, add some water or broth, as the soup will thicken after it sits in the refrigerator.

INGREDIENTS:

2 cups green lentils

5 cups water or low-sodium vegetable broth

1 15-ounce can diced tomatoes

1 tablespoon apple cider vinegar

2 shallots, finely chopped

1 tablespoon fresh ginger, peeled and grated

1½ teaspoons ground coriander

1½ teaspoon ground cumin

⅛ teaspoon ground cloves

1 teaspoon paprika

¼ teaspoon cayenne pepper

1 teaspoon salt, or to taste

1 cinnamon stick

4 cups tightly packed curly kale leaves

Golden raisins and plain yogurt for serving

Crock Pot Shredded Chicken Chili with Mushrooms and Kale

Serves 6.

INSTRUCTIONS:

1. In a large skillet, heat the oil to medium. Add the onion and sauté, stirring consistently, until it begins to turn brown, about 8 minutes.
2. Add the bell pepper and jalapeños and sauté another 3 minutes. Add the garlic and mushrooms and sauté until the mushrooms begin turning brown and soften, about another 5 minutes.
3. Add the diced tomatoes to the bottom of the crock pot, then place the raw chicken on top. Pour the vegetable sauté mixture over the chicken.
4. In a small bowl, mix together all of the spices. Add the chicken stock, beans, and the spice mixture to the crock pot and stir well. Cover and place on the low setting for 8 hours.
5. One hour before finished cooking, add the chopped kale leaves and mix in.
6. Serve chili with sour cream or plain Greek yogurt and your other favorite chili toppings.

INGREDIENTS:

1 tablespoon olive oil

1 yellow onion, chopped

1 red bell pepper, chopped

2 jalapeno peppers, seeded and chopped

6 cloves garlic, minced

8 to 10 crimini mushrooms, chopped into sixths

1 28-ounce can diced tomatoes

2 boneless, skinless chicken breasts

2 cups low-sodium chicken broth

1 14-ounce can black beans

½ teaspoon unsweetened cocoa powder

1 tablespoon smoked paprika

1 tablespoon ground cumin

¾ teaspoon ground sage

1 teaspoon dried oregano

½ teaspoon ground cayenne pepper

1 teaspoon kosher salt, or to taste

1 head kale, stems removed, leaves finely chopped

Hearty Vegetable Chili

Serves 6.

INSTRUCTIONS:

1. In a large pot, add 1 tablespoon of oil and heat to medium. Add the chopped eggplant and cook, stirring constantly, until the eggplant browns on the edges, about 3 minutes. Pour the eggplant into a large bowl and set aside.

2. Add the last tablespoon of oil to the same pot and keeping the heat on medium, sauté the onion until it begins to sweat and becomes fragrant, about 3 minutes. Add the bell pepper and garlic and sauté until veggies are softened, about 5 to 8 minutes.

3. Add the chopped zucchini and sauté an additional 3 to 5 minutes. Add the eggplant and the rest of the ingredients except for the kale. Stir well to combine. Bring the chili to a boil, then immediately reduce the heat to medium–low, cover the pot, and allow chili to simmer for 15 minutes.

4. A few minutes before you're ready to serve the chili, add the chopped kale leaves and cover the pot to allow them to steam and soften.

5. Serve the chili with all of your favorite toppings!

INGREDIENTS:

1 eggplant, chopped into ½" squares

2 tablespoons grapeseed or olive oil, divided

1 large yellow onion, chopped

1 green bell pepper, chopped

4 cloves garlic, minced

2 medium zucchini squash

1 28-ounce can diced tomatoes

1 14-ounce can pinto beans

1 14-ounce can black beans

1 cup vegetable broth (or water)

2 tablespoons chili powder

½ teaspoon ground cumin

1 teaspoon fresh oregano, finely chopped (or ½ teaspoon dried oregano)

½ teaspoon salt, or to taste

5 to 6 cups tightly packed dino kale leaves, chopped

Indian Chickpea Stew with Kale

Serves 6 to 8.

Instructions:

1. In a large pot or Dutch oven, sauté the onion over medium heat until it begins to brown, about 8 to 10 minutes.

2. Add all of the ingredients except for the kale and stir to combine. Cover and bring the pot to a boil.

3. Once a full boil is reached, lower the heat to medium-low and allow the stew to cook at a gentle boil about 15 minutes.

4. Remove the cover from the pot and add all of the kale. It's okay if the pot is very full at this point; the kale will cook down.

5. Put the cover back on and allow the kale to steam about 30 seconds to 1 minute before stirring it into the stew to incorporate it.

6. Cook an additional 2 minutes, then serve over cooked brown rice.

Ingredients:

1 tablespoon olive or grapeseed oil

1 large yellow onion, chopped

4 cloves garlic, minced

1 28-ounce can diced tomatoes, including juices

2 15-ounce cans garbanzo beans, drained and rinsed

3 cups vegetable broth (low-sodium kind recommended)

1½ teaspoons turmeric

2 teaspoons ground cumin

1 teaspoon coriander

2 teaspoons fresh ginger, peeled and grated

½ teaspoon salt, or to taste

1 bay leaf

8 cups green kale leaves, stems removed, chopped

Brown rice for serving

Kale and White Bean Soup

Serves 4 to 6.

INSTRUCTIONS:

1. In a large stock pot or Dutch oven, heat the oil to medium.
2. Add the chopped yam and sauté 2 minutes before adding the onion, carrot, and celery.
3. Continue sautéing vegetables until onion is transluscent and yam is softened but still al dente, about 8 to 10 minutes.
4. Add the thyme, cumin, and salts and sauté one minute before adding the chicken broth.
5. Bring the soup to a full boil. Reduce the heat to a simmer, and cook covered about 15 to 20 minutes until all veggies are cooked all the way through.
6. Add the white beans and kale and continue to simmer, covered, until kale is softened and wilted, about 3 to 5 minutes.
7. Serve with rustic, crusty bread and enjoy!

INGREDIENTS:

2 tablespoons olive oil

1 large yellow onion, chopped

2 carrots, peeled and chopped

1 small yam (or sweet potato), peeled and chopped (about 2 cups worth)

2 celery stocks, chopped

½ teaspoon salt, or to taste

½ teaspoon thyme leaves

1 teaspoon ground cumin

½ teaspoons kosher salt, or to taste

6 cups low sodium chicken broth

1 15.5-ounce can white (cannellini) beans, drained and rinsed

6 cups tightly packed green curly kale leaves, chopped

Minestrone Soup with Quinoa

Serves 6 to 8.

INSTRUCTIONS:

1. In a large stock pot or Dutch oven, add oil and heat to medium. Add the chopped onion and sauté until fragrant and softened, about 3 minutes.
2. Add the carrots, celery, and red potatoes. Continue sautéing, stirring frequently, until vegetables have softened but are still al dente, about 8 minutes.
3. Add the garlic, green beans, and spices and sauté another 1 minute. Add the diced tomatoes, chicken broth, quinoa, and parmesan cheese rind. Bring the soup to a full boil, then reduce the heat to a simmer. Cover the pot and cook for 30 minutes or until vegetables are cooked through and quinoa is cooked.
4. Add the cannellini beans and kale leaves. Cook an additional 8 minutes or until kale leaves are softened.
5. Remove the parmesan rind. Serve with rustic toasted bread and shredded parmesan cheese on top.

INGREDIENTS:

3 tablespoons olive oil

1 yellow onion, chopped

2 carrots, peeled and chopped

3 stalks celery, chopped

2 red potatoes, chopped

6 cloves garlic, minced

3 cups green beans, chopped into 1½" pieces

1 teaspoon dried basil

½ teaspoon dried oregano

¼ teaspoon dried thyme

½ teaspoon ground sage

2 14.5-ounce cans diced tomatoes

6 cups low-sodium chicken broth

¾ cup uncooked quinoa

1 rind parmesan cheese

1 14-ounce can cannellini beans, drained and rinsed

1 head dino kale leaves, chopped

¾ teaspoon kosher salt, or to taste

Parmesan cheese for serving

Smoked Paprika Chicken Corn Chowder

INSTRUCTIONS:

1. In a large pot or Dutch oven, add the oil and heat to medium.
2. Add the yellow onion, carrots, and celery. Sauté, stirring frequently, until the vegetables have softened but are still al dente, about 15 minutes. Add the garlic and corn and saute another 5 minutes.
3. Add the broth, cream, and paprika, and stir everything together. Bring pot to a full boil.
4. In a small cup, mix together the brown rice flour and the water until all the lumps are out. Pour this mixture into the soup. Add the raw chopped chicken to the soup and return soup to a boil.
5. Reduce the heat to medium-low and allow the soup to boil gently, uncovered, for 20 to 30 minutes, or until chicken and vegetables are cooked through.
6. Add the kale leaves, stir them into the soup, and cover the pot. Cook for 5 to 8 minutes, or until kale leaves have softened and wilted.

INGREDIENTS:

2 tablespoons grapeseed or olive oil

1 large yellow onion, chopped

2 carrots, peeled and chopped

2 stalks celery, chopped

6 cloves garlic, minced

4 ears white sweet corn, kernels removed

1 quart chicken broth

1 cup cream (or coconut milk)

2 tablespoons Hungarian paprika

2 tablespoons brown rice flour (or regular flour)

½ cup water

1½ pounds chicken, chopped into cubes

6 cups tightly packed kale leaves, chopped

Thai Coconut Soup with Brown Rice and Chicken

Serves 4.

INSTRUCTIONS:

1. Smash the lemongrass stalks and peel the outer layers. Slice the stalks lengthwise, then chop them into 2" to 3" pieces.

2. Heat the oil in a pot or Dutch oven to medium and add the lemongrass. Sauté the lemongrass stalks until very fragrant, about 3 to 5 minutes.

3. Add the red sweet peppers, brown rice, and ginger. Sauté until peppers and ginger are very fragrant, about 3 minutes. Add the chopped chicken and stir quickly to slightly brown the chicken, about 30 seconds (don't cook through).

4. Add the chicken broth, coconut milk, lime juice, and fish sauce. Bring the soup to a full boil. Reduce heat to medium–low, cover the pot, and allow soup to simmer about 30 minutes, or until chicken and rice are cooked through.

5. Add the chopped kale leaves and stir them into the soup. Cover the pot and cook until leaves have softened, about 5 minutes.

6. Prior to serving the soup, use a slotted spoon to remove the lemongrass stalks from the soup (or warn your guests to pick out the stalks, as they are difficult to chew).

7. Serve the soup with fresh chopped cilantro.

INGREDIENTS:

2 tablespoons coconut oil or grapeseed oil

3 stalks lemongrass

3 small red sweet peppers (or red chilies or bell peppers), chopped

½ cup uncooked brown rice

1 teaspoon ground ginger (or 1 tablespoon fresh ginger, peeled and grated)

1 pound boneless, skinless chicken breasts, chopped*

6 cups chicken broth

1 14-ounce can coconut milk (full fat recommended)

3 limes, juiced

3 tablespoons fish sauce

4 to 6 cups green curly kale leaves, chopped

Cilantro for serving

*You can also use roasted chicken (about 4 cups worth)

Sausage, Fennel, and Kale Soup

Serves 4.

INSTRUCTIONS:

1. In a large stock pot or Dutch oven, heat oil to medium.
2. Add the potatoes and sauté about 2 minutes before adding the onion, fennel, ground ginger, cumin, and salt.
3. Sauté veggies until softened, about 10 minutes.
4. Add the chicken broth and bring to a full boil. Reduce heat to a simmer and cook covered for 15 minutes, or until vegetables are softened and cooked all the way through.
5. While the soup is simmering, put your oven on the high broil setting.
6. Place the two sausages in a casserole dish and broil them on one side for 5 minutes (or until browned and crispy) before flipping them to the other side and broiling an additional 5 minutes, or until cooked all the way through (you can check whether the sausage is cooked through by poking it with your finger. If the sausage feels firm, it is cooked).
7. Allow the sausages to cool enough to handle and then slice them. Add the sausage to the soup.
8. Add the chopped kale leaves and stir them into the soup. Cook covered until leaves have wilted and are softened, about 5 minutes.
9. Serve soup with crusty rustic bread.

INGREDIENTS:

2 tablespoons grapeseed or olive oil
2 cups red potato, chopped (about 2 small red potatoes)
1 large yellow onion, chopped
1 bulb fennel, chopped (about 3 cups)
½ teaspoon ground ginger
1 teaspoon ground cumin
¾ teaspoon salt, or to taste
1 quart low-sodium chicken broth
4 to 6 cups curly green kale leaves, chopped
2 turkey Italian sausages, broiled and sliced

Main Dishes

Barbecue Black Bean, Kale, and Sweet Potato Veggie Burgers

Makes 6 burger patties.

INSTRUCTIONS:

1. Place one can of black beans in a food processor and pulse a few times to mash the beans but leave them slightly chunky. Pour this mixture into a mixing bowl. Add the remaining ingredients to the mixing bowl and stir to combine.
2. Heat a cast iron skillet to medium–high and add enough oil to coat the bottom of the pan.
3. Form patties out of the veggie mixture. Place patties on the hot skillet and cook until the sides begin to firm up, about 3 to 4 minutes.
4. Carefully flip the patties and cook until the patty is firm when poked. Both sides of the patty should be crisp.
5. Toast hamburger buns cut-side up in the oven on broil. Add your favorite toppings to the burger, such as avocado slices, tomato, red onion, etc.

INGREDIENTS:

2 14-ounce cans black beans, drained and rinsed
1½ cups sweet potato, roasted and chopped/lightly mashed
2 cups kale leaves, finely chopped
½ cup brown rice flour
¼ cup green onion, chopped
1 egg, lightly beaten
1 tablespoon barbecue sauce
¼ teaspoon salt
1½ teaspoons paprika
2 teaspoons chili powder
½ teaspoon garlic powder
Pinch cayenne pepper, optional
1 to 2 tablespoons olive oil for cooking

Serving Suggestions:
Toasted bun, red onion, avocado, and barbecue sauce

Let Them Eat Kale! 139

Blackened Salmon with Garlicy Cajun Kale

Serves 2.

INSTRUCTIONS:

1. Heat the oil in a 10" cast iron skillet to just over medium heat until the oil is smoking.
2. Carefully place the salmon flesh-down on the skillet and cook for about 3 minutes. Using a spatula, carefully flip the fillet to the skin side and cook another 6 minutes, or just until cooked through. Remove the cast iron skillet from the heat and place the fillet on a plate.
3. Allow the skillet to cool until it's no longer smoking. Place the skillet back on the burner over low heat. Add the garlic, ginger, and kale and sauté, stirring constantly until kale has softened and is wilted, about 4 to 5 minutes.
4. Sprinkle with salt to taste and grate fresh lemon zest over the kale. Serve kale and salmon together with lemon wedges.

INGREDIENTS:

For the Salmon Fillet:

1½ tablespoons almond oil*

½ to ¾ pound salmon fillet

1 tablespoon Cajun seasoning (see recipe below)

For the Garlicy Cajun Kale:

1 head dino kale

5 cloves garlic, minced

Zest of 1 lemon

½ teaspoon Cajun seasoning

Cajun Seasoning:

2 teaspoons kosher salt

3 teaspoons garlic powder

1 teaspoon onion powder

4 teaspoons smoked paprika

1 teaspoon dried oregano

¾ teaspoon ground sage

¾ teaspoon ground black pepper

1 teaspoon ground cayenne pepper

*Or high temperature oil of choice, such as canola

Cauliflower and Kale Yellow Curry

Serves 4 to 6.

INSTRUCTIONS:

1. In a large skillet, heat ½ cup of the coconut milk over medium heat and add the chopped onion. Sauté the onion until it begins to soften, about 3 minutes.

2. Add the red potato and continue sautéing until the potato has softened but is still al dente, about 10 minutes. Add small amounts of coconut milk if pan ever becomes dry.

3. Add the garlic, ginger, cumin, turmeric, coriander, and another ½ cup of coconut milk. Sauté until the ginger and garlic are fragrant, about 3 minutes.

4. Add the cauliflower, green beans, and remaining coconut milk. Stir together well, cover, and stir every few minutes until vegetables are cooked through, about 10 to 15 minutes.

5. Add the kale leaves on top of the curry, replace the cover, and allow kale to steam until softened, about 3 minutes. Mix the kale into the curry, drizzle lime juice over everything, and serve over cooked brown rice.

INGREDIENTS:

3 cups full-fat canned coconut milk, divided

1 yellow onion, chopped

2 red potatoes, chopped into ½" pieces

6 cloves garlic, minced

2 teaspoons fresh grated ginger

1 tablespoon ground cumin

2 teaspoons turmeric

1 teaspoon ground coriander

½ head cauliflower, chopped into florets

2 cups green beans, chopped

4 cups green kale leaves, chopped

1 lime, juiced

Cooked brown rice for serving

Vegetable curry is one of my favorite applications for kale. I love combining a variety of vegetables with yellow curry-spiced coconut milk to make a filling and completely healthful meal. This recipe comes together quickly, making it the perfect meal to assemble any night of the week.

Chicken and Kale Burrito Bowls

Serves 3 to 4.

INSTRUCTIONS:

1. Preheat the oven to 350 degrees F. In a small bowl, mix together the oil, cumin, chili powder, and salt. Pour this mixture over the chicken and gently rub it into the chicken. Allow the chicken to marinate for 15 minutes. Place the chicken in a casserole dish and bake it in the oven for 35 to 40 minutes, or until the internal temperature is 160 degrees F.

2. Remove the chicken from the oven and allow it to cool slightly. Using two forks, shred the chicken into long strips (you can also chop the chicken). Set aside until ready to use.

3. While the chicken is cooking, heat 2 cups of water in a small pot until boiling. Add rice and return the water to a boil. Reduce the heat to medium-low, cover the pot, and cook until all of the water has been absorbed, about 35 to 40 minutes (or follow cook time on the package).

4. Rinse the kale leaves well, but don't pat them dry, leaving some water on them. Chop the leaves, place them in a large skillet, and place skillet on the stove over medium-low to medium heat. Allow kale to cook, removing the lid a few times to stir, until wilted, about 5 to 8 minutes.

5. Heat the beans in a small pot until they begin to bubble. Make your burrito bowls by adding desired amount of kale, rice, beans, chicken, pico de gallo, and guacamole to each bowl.

INGREDIENTS:

1 boneless, skinless chicken breast*

1 tablespoon olive oil

1 teaspoon cumin

1 teaspoon chili powder

¼ teaspoon kosher salt

1 cup brown rice

1 head curly kale, stems removed, leaves chopped

1 14-ounce can black beans

Pico de gallo (from pg. 189)

Guacamole (from pg. 185)

Cheese for serving, optional

*You can also use roast chicken

Chili Verde Shredded Chicken Enchiladas

Makes 6 enchiladas.

INSTRUCTIONS:

1. In a Dutch oven or large pot, heat oil over medium heat. Add the red onion and sauté one minute before adding bell pepper. Sauté until veggies have softened slightly, about 3 minutes.
2. Place the chicken breast in the pot on top of the veggies and cover with 2 cups of green salsa. Cover the pot, reduce heat to medium–low, and allow mixture to gently bubble for 12 minutes. Uncover the pot, flip the chicken to the other side, replace the cover, and cook an additional 8 minutes, or until cooked all the way through.
3. Add the chopped kale, cover, and allow the kale to soften, about 2 to 3 minutes.
4. Remove pot from the heat and using a fork, place chicken breast on a cutting board. Using two forks, shred the chicken. Add chicken back to the pot with the onion, pepper, and kale and mix everything together.
5. Preheat the oven to 415 degrees F.
6. Pour a small amount of green salsa in a casserole dish and spread it to coat the bottom.
7. Fill tortillas with the chicken and kale mixture, roll them up, and place them close together in the casserole dish. Cover with the remaining green salsa and cheese. Bake for 12 to 15 minutes or until cheese is melted and slightly browned. Serve with olives and other desired toppings on top.

INGREDIENTS:

2 tablespoons grapeseed or olive oil

½ red onion, chopped

1 green bell pepper, chopped

3 cloves garlic, minced

1 boneless, skinless chicken breast

5 cups green (tomatillo) salsa, divided (see pg. 197)

4 cups tightly packed kale leaves, chopped

6 large flour tortillas

1½ cups shredded pepper jack cheese

For Serving:

Black olives

Green onion

Sour cream

Avocado

Creamy Portobello and Kale Quinoa Bake

Serves 8 to 10.

INSTRUCTIONS:

1. Rinse the quinoa well until the water that comes off of it is clear. Add the quinoa and 4 cups of water to a medium-sized pot and bring to a full boil. Reduce the heat and simmer covered until all of the water is absorbed, about 20 minutes. Remove the quinoa from the heat, fluff it with a fork. Add the half-and-half, ricotta cheese, and parmesan cheese to the hot quinoa and gently fold everything together. Set aside.

2. Add the olive oil to a large skillet and heat to medium. Add the onion and sauté until it begins to brown, about 15 minutes. Add the sliced portobello mushrooms and continue sautéing until mushrooms are deep brown and soft, about 10 to 15 minutes. Add the garlic and thyme and sauté another minute.

3. Add the diced tomatoes and bring mixture to a gentle boil. Cook until much of the liquid has cooked off (you want this to be a chunky sauce with only a small amount of liquid). Add the chopped kale leaves, cover the skillet, and cook until leaves have softened and wilted, about 3 to 5 minutes. Pour the mushroom/kale mixture into the pot with the quinoa and gently fold all of the ingredients together.

4. Preheat the oven to 400 degrees F and lightly oil a casserole dish. Pour the quinoa mixture into the casserole dish and spread it around so that it is evenly distributed. Sprinkle the shredded mozzarella and gouda cheese on top and bake in the oven until cheese has melted and begins turning brown, about 10 to 15 minutes. Serve as a main dish or a side dish!

INGREDIENTS:

2 cups uncooked quinoa

3 tablespoons olive oil

1 yellow onion, chopped

5 portobello mushrooms, sliced ¼" thick

8 cloves garlic, minced

2 teaspoons fresh thyme

1 28-ounce can diced tomatoes

1 head dino kale, leaves chopped

1 teaspoon salt

½ cup half-and-half or cream

½ cup ricotta cheese

¾ cup grated parmesan cheese

2 cups shredded mozzarella cheese

1 cup shredded gouda cheese

Eggplant, Kale, and Chickpea Tacos with Charmoula Sauce

Serves 3 to 4.

INSTRUCTIONS:

1. In a large sauté pan, heat the olive oil and butter over medium heat.
2. Add the eggplant and use a spatula to toss the eggplant in the oil/butter to evenly coat. Sauté until eggplant begins turning brown, about 3 minutes.
3. Add the chopped garlic and chickpeas. Continue sautéing, stirring consistently until eggplant is very brown and begins losing its form, about 5 to 8 minutes.
4. Add the chopped kale and continue sautéing and stirring until kale has softened, about 5 minutes.
5. In a small separate skillet, heat tortillas one or two at a time over medium heat until warm.
6. Add desired amount of veggie mixture to tortillas and drizzle Charmoula sauce on top.

INGREDIENTS:

3 tablespoons olive oil

1 tablespoon unsalted butter

1 eggplant, unpeeled, chopped into strips (unpeeled)

6 cloves garlic

1 14-ounce can chickpeas, drained and rinsed

1 head dino kale

½ teaspoon kosher salt

6 to 8 corn or flour tortillas

Charmoula sauce (pg. 181)

These Middle Eastern-inspired tacos are packed with flavor and nutrition. Using the Charmoula sauce from the sauces section of this book adds an earthy and zesty flavor to the buttery vegetarian taco filling. As an alternative to tacos, this mixture can be served on rustic toasted bread as an appetizer, or on its own as a vegetable side dish.

Turkey Sausage, Bell Pepper, Mushroom Pizza on Spinach and Kale Crust (gluten & grain-free pizza crust)

Serves 4.

INGREDIENTS:

For Kale and Spinach "Pizza Crust":

1 pound bag frozen chopped kale

1 pound bag frozen chopped spinach

4 eggs

5 cloves garlic, minced

Recipe makes two 13" round pizzas, or one baking sheet pizza

For the Pizza Sauce:

6 large tomatoes (or 2 14-ounce cans diced tomatoes)

5 cloves garlic, minced

½ yellow onion, finely chopped

8 large basil leaves, chopped

2 tablespoons chopped fresh parsley

Dash of salt and pepper

Pinch of cayenne pepper

Suggested Toppings:

1 cup ground turkey Italian sausage, cooked

8 ounces mozzarella cheese, shredded

8 baby bella mushrooms

1 red bell pepper, thinly sliced lengthwise

2 tablespoons sun-dried tomatoes

Continued on next page . . .

It may seem strange to build a pizza on kale and spinach, but greens make an incredibly tasty crust! This nutritious and gluten-free crust can be used to make your favorite pizza, or cut into squares for making sandwiches or paninis.

INSTRUCTIONS:

For the Pizza Crust:

1. Preheat the oven to 350 degrees F and spread the frozen chopped kale and spinach on a cookie sheet. Bake in the oven for 10 minutes, enough time to thaw the greens. Remove the kale and spinach from the oven and squeeze the water out of them; you can put the greens in a cheesecloth for this step or use just your hands.

2. While the greens are thawing in the oven, heat the butter in a skillet over medium heat. Add the garlic and sun-dried tomatoes and cook just until garlic is fragrant and softened, about 3 minutes. Remove from heat and set aside to cool.

3. Beat the eggs in a medium-sized mixing bowl. Place the greens in the mixing bowl with the egg. Add the sautéed garlic and sun-dried tomatoes into the mixing bowl and mix all ingredients well, ensuring the eggs are well incorporated.

4. Increase oven heat to 375 degrees F. Place a sheet of parchment paper on top of your pizza trays. If you don't have pizza trays, it is perfectly acceptable to use a large cookie sheet instead. Pour the green mixture onto the parchment paper and with a fork or your fingers, pat down the greens until the entire pizza tray is evenly covered. Place both pizza crusts in the oven and bake for 30 to 35 minutes until the edges are barely beginning to crisp and the crust feels firm.

For the Pizza Sauce:

1. While the pizza crust is baking, assemble your pizza sauce. Over medium heat, sauté the onion and garlic until fragrant and soft. Add the coarsely chopped tomatoes, bring to a slight boil, then turn heat to low. Add basil, parsley, salt, pepper, and cayenne pepper and simmer covered while the pizza crust is baking, stirring occasionally, about 30 minutes.

To Prepare the Pizzas:

1. Heat the sun-dried tomatoes in 1 tablespoon of oil over medium heat. Once warm, add the red bell pepper and mushroom slices and sauté until fragrant and beginning to soften, about 2 minutes. Add the turkey sausage and allow it to brown on all sides. You do not need to let the sausage cook all the way through, as it will continue to cook in the oven. Remove from heat.

2. Turn oven heat up to 400 degrees F. Assemble your pizzas, adding sauce first. Sprinkle mozzarella cheese liberally and arrange your red bell pepper, mushrooms, sun-dried tomatoes, and sausage on top. Place pizzas in the oven and bake for 10 minutes until cheese is fully melted and toppings have reached the desired crispness.

Indian Lamb Curry with Kale

Serves 4 to 6.

INSTRUCTIONS:

1. In a large pot or Dutch oven, heat the oil to medium and sauté the onion until it begins to turn translucent, about 8 minutes.
2. Add the garlic and fresh ginger and sauté an additional 3 minutes.
3. Add the lamb stew meat and allow it to brown slightly but do not cook it all the way through. Add the coconut milk and curry powder and stir well to combine everything.
4. Bring the curry to a gentle boil and then reduce the heat to medium–low. Allow it to simmer, covered, for 15 minutes, or until lamb is cooked but still tender.
5. Add the chopped kale leaves, mix them into the curry, and cover the pot to allow the leaves to steam and soften, about 3 to 4 minutes.
6. Serve the curry over rice.

INGREDIENTS:

2 tablespoons grapeseed or olive oil

1 large yellow onion, chopped

6 cloves garlic, minced

2 tablespoons fresh ginger, peeled and finely grated

3 pounds lamb stew meat

1 14-ounce can full-fat coconut milk

3 tablespoons yellow curry powder

2 to 3 cups tightly packed green kale leaves, chopped

Rice for serving

Lemony Braised Chicken and Kale

INSTRUCTIONS:

1. Butcher the chicken into pieces.
2. Heat 2 tablespoons of the oil in a large cast iron skillet to medium–high heat.
3. Sprinkle the raw chicken pieces with salt and pepper. Place the pieces of chicken skin-side down on the cast iron skillet. Cook until the chicken becomes crispy and browned, about 8 minutes. Flip chicken to the other side and cook another 2 to 3 minutes, but do not cook the chicken all the way through. Put chicken pieces on a plate and set aside.
4. Preheat the oven to 425 degrees F.
5. In a Dutch oven or all-metal or cast iron pot, heat 1 tablespoon of oil over medium heat on the stovetop. Add the chopped onion and sauté until translucent, about 8 minutes. Add the garlic and sauté another couple of minutes.
6. Arrange the pieces of chicken in the pot so that they are skin-side up. Pour the chicken broth, wine, lemon juice, and lemon zest over the chicken.
7. Cover the pot and place it in the oven. Allow chicken to cook for 20 to 25 minutes until the chicken breasts reach 160 dgrees F and the thigh pieces reach 180 degrees F.
8. Five minutes before the chicken is ready, remove the pot from the oven, add the kale leaves, stir them into the chicken and broth, and place the pot back in the oven. Allow the leaves to steam for 5 minutes, stirring once if desired. Carefully remove the pot from the oven. Scoop kale and chicken onto plates and spoon the broth over the food. The broth gives the meal a great deal of flavor.

INGREDIENTS:

1 whole chicken

3 tablespoons grapeseed or canola oil, divided

1 large yellow onion, chopped

6 cloves garlic, minced

2 cups low-sodium chicken broth

1 cup dry white wine, such as chardonnay or sauvignon blanc

1 whole lemon, zested and juiced

1 head green kale, leaves chopped

Salt and pepper to taste

Sautéed Shrimp and Kale Tacos with Pineapple, Corn, and Kale Salsa

Serves 3 to 4.

INSTRUCTIONS:

1. Add olive oil and butter to a skillet and heat to medium-high.
2. Add garlic, ginger, curry powder, paprika, and salt and cook sauté one minute before adding shrimp. Cook the shrimp about 1 to 2 minutes on each side until they turn pink and are cooked all the way through. Add the chopped kale leaves in with the shrimp and cover the skillet, allowing the kale leaves to steam and soften, about 1 to 2 minutes.
3. Wrap the corn tortillas in foil and heat them in the oven at 350 degrees F, until warm.
4. Assemble the tacos by adding desired amount of kale, shrimp, Pineapple-Corn-Kale Salsa, and your other favorite taco toppings.

INGREDIENTS:

1 tablespoon olive oil
1 tablespoon butter
1 pound shrimp, peeled
1 head green curly kale, stems removed, leaves chopped
5 cloves garlic, minced
2 teaspoons fresh ginger, peeled and grated
3 teaspoons yellow curry powder
½ teaspoon paprika
Pinch of salt

For Serving:
Pineapple, Corn, and Kale Salsa (pg. 191)
Avocado
Corn tortillas

Shrimp, Artichoke Heart, Sun-Dried Tomato Pesto Pizza

Makes one 12-inch pizza.

INSTRUCTIONS:

For Preparing the Pizza Dough:

1. Pour ¾ cup warm water in a bowl. The water should feel slightly warm to the touch and should be no higher than 100 degrees F, and no less than 80 degrees F.
2. Add the packet of yeast and mix using a fork.
3. Add ¼ cup of the all-purpose flour and mix until all chunks disappear. Allow this mixture to sit for 15 minutes with a towel covering the bowl. This process gives the yeast time to activate and some food to munch on to make it happy.
4. Add 1 cup of flour to the yeast and mix thoroughly.
5. Begin adding the remaining flour, ¼ cup at a time and mixing until incorporated. By now, the dough should be forming and moving away from the sides of the bowl. If it is still too sticky to grab with your hands, dust a little more flour on the dough.

Continued on next page . . .

INGREDIENTS:

For the Pizza Crust:

¾ cup warm water (around 100 degrees F).
1 packet dry yeast
1 teaspoon salt
2¼ cup gluten-free all-purpose flour, plus more for dusting

For the Pizza Toppings:

1 tablespoon olive oil
¼ to ½ pound raw shrimp, shelled
Juice of 1 lemon
4 cloves garlic
⅓ cup pesto sauce
½ cup artichoke hearts
¼ cup julienne cut sun-dried tomatoes
1¼ cups shredded mozzarella cheese

6. Turn dough out onto a floured surface and knead for a minute or so. The dough needs to stay soft and not get too tough, so don't overzealously knead. You should end up with a ball of dough that does not stick to your hands but also does not crumble apart.

7. Coat the ball of dough with a little olive oil and place it in a large mixing bowl with a towel over it. Allow dough to sit 30 minutes.

8. Preheat the oven to 375 degrees F.

9. Prepare a pizza tray or baking dish by coating it lightly with olive oil.

10. Remove dough from bowl, knead for about 30 seconds, then either roll the dough out or press it into a 12" pizza tray or baking dish using your hands. If the dough gets craggly around the edges, simply smooth it out by pressing it together.

11. Bake the dough for 15 to 18 minutes, or until it begins to turn golden brown on the edges and feels firm to the touch.

12. Remove pizza crust from the oven, leaving the oven at 375 degrees F, and build your pizza.

To Prepare the Pizza:

1. In a small skillet, heat the oil to medium and add the shrimp, garlic, and lemon juice. Allow shrimp to cook on one side for about 1 to 2 minutes, or until the sides begin to firm up. Flip shrimp to the other side and continue cooking another minute or two, or until the shrimp are cooked through.

2. Spread the pesto sauce over the pizza crust, then add the sun-dried tomatoes, cheese, artichoke hearts, and shrimp.

3. Bake for 15 to 20 minutes, or until the cheese is melted and beginning to brown, and the crust is crispy.

4. Allow the pizza to cool 8 to 10 minutes before slicing and serving it up.

Spaghetti Squash with Spicy Mushroom, Roasted Garlic, and Kale Sauce

Serves 4.

INSTRUCTIONS:

To Prepare the Spaghetti Squash:

1. Preheat the oven to 400 degrees F.
2. Chop the tip and the tail off of the spaghetti squash, cut it in half lengthwise, and scoop the seeds out of each half.
3. Rub about a tablespoon of olive oil over the flesh of each half. Sprinkle with salt and pepper. Place the squash cut-side down on a baking sheet.
4. Chop the tops off of each bulb of garlic and drizzle olive oil over the exposed cloves. Wrap each bulb in foil and place on the baking sheet with the spaghetti squash. Roast the squash and garlic for 45 to 50 minutes.
5. When the squash is cool enough to handle, use a fork to gently scrape the flesh, releasing spaghetti-like stands. Do this until both halves of the spaghetti squash are scraped clean and place the "spaghetti" into a large serving bowl.

To Prepare the Spicy Sauce:

1. While the squash is roasting, prepare the sauce. In a large skillet, heat 2 tablespoons of olive oil over medium heat.

INGREDIENTS:

1 spaghetti squash

2 garlic bulbs

For the Sauce:

2 tablespoons olive oil

1 yellow onion, chopped

10 crimini mushrooms, chopped into sixths

1 28-ounce can diced tomatoes

⅓ cup vegetable or chicken broth (or water)

1 teaspoon oregano

½ teaspoon dried rosemary

1 teaspoon ground sage

½ teaspoon ground cayenne

1 teaspoon salt

1 head of dino kale, chopped

1 tablespoon fresh basil leaves, chopped

Continued on next page . . .

2. Add the onion and sauté, stirring consistently until onion begins to turn brown, about 8 minutes. Add the chopped mushrooms and continue sautéing until the mushrooms begin to cook down and are browned, about another 8 minutes.

3. Add the remaining ingredients except for the kale and basil and stir together. Bring sauce to a full boil.

4. Reduce heat to a gentle boil and cook covered for 45 minutes.

5. Remove the cover, add the chopped kale and basil leaves, replace the cover, and simmer an additional 10 to 15 minutes.

6. Serve the spaghetti squash with desired amount of sauce on top along with rustic bread.

Note: You can also add chicken to this recipe for some animal protein.

The ingredients for this sauce are very simple, and yet it comes out packed with flavor. For those who are gluten-intolerant or simply like to limit gluten, spaghetti squash is a great alternative to pasta.

Roasted Portobello Mushrooms with Eggplant Caponata

INSTRUCTIONS:

1. In a large skillet, heat ½ cup of the olive oil to medium and add the chopped eggplant. Toss the eggplant to evenly coat in oil. Saute, stirring frequently, until eggplant has browned, begins cooking down, and is soft, about 10 minutes. Pour the eggplant into a bowl and set aside.

2. Place the skillet back on the stove and add ¼ cup of oil. Add the onion and celery and sauté, stirring every couple of minutes, until veggies are cooked through, about 10 minutes. Add the garlic and sauté another 2 minutes.

3. Add the raisins, capers, olives, diced tomatoes, vinegar, salt, and remaining oil. Bring mixture to a full boil, reduce the heat, and allow the sauce to boil gently (uncovered) until much of the liquid has been reduced, about 15 minutes. Add the parsley, kale, and basil and stir everything together well. Cook until kale has wilted, about 5 to 8 minutes.

4. While the caponata is simmering, prepare the roasted mushrooms. Preheat the oven to 350 degrees F. Remove the stems from the mushrooms and lightly oil them. Place them on a parchment-lined baking sheet and bake for 25 to 30 minutes, or until mushrooms are soft, fragrant, and dark juices are seeping out. Pile desired amount of hot eggplant caponata on the mushrooms. Serve as a side dish or as a main dish with bread and salad.

INGREDIENTS:

6 portobello mushrooms

Olive oil

Salt and pepper

For the Caponata:

2 cups olive oil, divided

1 large eggplant, peeled and chopped into 1" cubes

1 yellow onion, chopped

2 celery stalks, chopped

6 cloves garlic, minced

½ cup raisins

2 tablespoons capers

⅔ cup pitted Kalamata olives, halved

1 14-ounce can diced tomatoes

¼ cup red wine vinegar

½ teaspoon salt

½ cup fresh parsley, chopped

¼ cup fresh basil, chopped

1 head lacinato kale, chopped

Sweet Potato Veggie Burritos with Coconut Curry Sauce

Makes 3 to 4 burritos.

INSTRUCTIONS:

1. In a bowl, mix together all of the ingredients for the coconut curry sauce until a uniform consistency is achieved. You can also blend all of the ingredients together in a blender.
2. Preheat the oven to 400 degrees F. Using a fork, poke holes in the sweet potato and then wrap it in foil. Place it on a baking sheet and roast it in the oven for 60 minutes, or until very soft.
3. Remove from the oven and allow potato to cool. When cool enough to handle, peel the skin off of the potato and mash the flesh using a fork.
4. While the potato is cooking, prepare the rice by bringing 2 cups of water to a boil. Add the rice to the boiling water, stir, and cover. Reduce the heat to medium-low and simmer for 35 to 40 minutes, or until water is absorbed (follow time instructions on your rice package).
5. In a small pot, heat the garbanzo beans until hot.
6. Heat the tortillas in a skillet over medium heat until warm (or wrap in foil and bake in the oven until warm).

INGREDIENTS:

For the Burritos:

1 large sweet potato, roasted

1 head kale, steamed

1 14-ounce can garbanzo beans

1 cup uncooked brown rice

3 to 4 large flour tortillas

For the Coconut Curry Sauce:

1 cup full-fat canned coconut milk

½ cup tahini

¼ cup + 1 tablespoon liquid aminos*

1 tablespoon curry powder, or to taste

¼ teaspoon salt

The thought of using a coconut curry sauce in a burrito as opposed to salsa may seem strange, but the coconut curry sauce pairs perfectly with the combination of vegetables in this burrito, and is absolutely delicious! This sauce can also be used for vegetable stir fry, as a dipping sauce, or as the perfect topping to a sweet potato veggie burger.

Vegetable Stir Fry with Turmeric Rice

Serves 3.

INSTRUCTIONS:

1. Rinse the rice well with water. In a pot, add the rinsed rice with the water (or broth) and salt. Allow the rice to sit for 15 minutes. Place the pot on the stove, covered, and bring it to a full boil. Immediately decrease the heat and add the turmeric. Stir, cover the pot again, and simmer for 35 minutes, or until the rice has absorbed all of the liquid.

2. In a wok or skillet, heat about 2 tablespoons of the sesame oil to medium-high. When the wok is all the way hot, add the onion and sauté, stirring constantly, until the onion softens but is still al dente (3 to 5 minutes). Pour the onion into a large bowl.

3. Add the cauliflower to the wok and turn down the heat to medium. Allow the cauliflower to cook, stirring every couple of minutes, until it has browned slightly but is still al dente, about 10 minutes. Add cauliflower to the bowl with the onion.

4. Add 1 tablespoon of sesame oil to the wok and add the green beans and mushrooms. Sauté until the veggies are soft and the mushrooms turn deep brown with a slight crisp on the outside, about 8 minutes. Add the green beans and mushrooms to the bowl with the other veggies.

5. Turn the heat down to medium-low and add the chopped kale leaves. Stir constantly until the kale leaves have wilted, about 3 minutes. Add the kale to the rest of the veggies. Add the remaining sesame oil, Thai chili, garlic, vinegar, honey, and fish sauce to the wok. Saute on medium-low until garlic is soft and fragrant, about 3 to 5 minutes. Pour this mixture over the vegetables and mix well. Serve stir fry vegetables over turmeric rice.

INGREDIENTS:

For the Stir Fry:

⅓ cup sesame oil, divided

1 red onion

½ head cauliflower

6 mushrooms, chopped

3 cups green beans, chopped into 1" pieces

1 head Russian red or green kale, chopped

1 Thai chili, seeds removed, finely chopped

8 cloves garlic, minced

2 tablespoons rice vinegar (or white vinegar)

2 teaspoons honey

2 tablespoons fish sauce

For the Rice:

1 cup basmati brown rice

2½ cups water*

½ teaspoon salt

½ teaspoon ground turmeric

*You can also use vegetable or chicken broth for more flavor.

Sauces, Salsa, and Spreads

Buttermilk Parsley Salad Dressing (or Dipping Sauce)

INSTRUCTIONS:

1. Add all ingredients to a blender or food processor and pulse until the parsley and kale have been chopped into small bits.
2. Pour the dressing into a sealable jar to use for salads or as dipping sauce for sweet potato fries (yum!). Dressing will keep for 10 to 14 days when sealed properly and refrigerated.

Note: You can also blend this dressing until completely smooth, but I like having small pieces of the parsley and kale.

INGREDIENTS:

2 cups buttermilk

1½ cups kale leaves, finely chopped

⅓ cup Greek yogurt

⅔ cup mayonnaise

⅓ cup olive oil

2 tablespoons green onion, chopped (about 1 stalk)

2 tablespoons flat leaf parsley, chopped

2 cloves garlic, minced

Zest of 1 lemon

2 tablespoons lemon juice

½ teaspoon kosher salt

Buttermilk parsley dressing is similar to ranch dressing, but this is a healthier version without all of the preservatives. If you are a mayonnaise-averse person, you can use more Greek yogurt and less mayo than the recipe calls for. The consistency of the dressing is dependent upon how much mayo versus how much Greek yogurt is used, but it turns out delicious every which way. It can be used for your favorite salads (try this on a cobb salad!), or it can double as a dipping sauce for baked sweet potato fries. This dressing requires very little effort—all you do is pour everything in a blender, flip the switch, and you have yourself a tasty dressing, with the world's favorite superfood, no less!

Charmoula Sauce

INSTRUCTIONS:

1. Add all ingredients to a blender or food processor and blend/process until a thick paste has formed. You can leave the sauce chunky or blend until completely smooth, depending on your preference.
2. If you don't have a blender or food processor, you can finely chop the first four ingredients and whisk everything together until well combined.

INGREDIENTS:

1 cup parsley

1 cup cilantro

1 cup dino kale leaves

6 to 8 cloves garlic

2 teaspoons kosher salt

1 tablespoon smoked paprika

2 teaspoons ground cumin

1 teaspoon ground coriander

¼ teaspoon cayenne pepper

½ cup olive oil

½ cup fresh lemon juice
(about 4 lemons, juiced)

Charmoula sauce is a traditional Middle Eastern sauce, typically made with parsley, cilantro, lemon juice, and Middle Eastern spices. It is used to marinate fish and poultry, or served on top of cooked meat and/or vegetables. All ingredients combined make for a sauce that is not only full of nutrients but also helps cleanse the liver.

Chimichurri Sauce

Makes 1 cup of sauce.

INSTRUCTIONS:

1. Add all ingredients except for oil to a blender or food processor.
2. Turn blender/processor on a low speed to chop the ingredients. Slowly add the oil while the machine is on.
3. Pour chimichurri sauce into a jar and seal to use for up to 1 week or use immediately.

Note: This sauce is perfect for steak, fajitas, salads, burgers, etc.

INGREDIENTS:

2 cups tightly packed flat leaf parsley

1 cup tightly packed green kale leaves

½ cup loosely packed fresh oregano leaves

5 cloves garlic, roughly chopped

Zest of 1 lime

2 tablespoons fresh lime juice

1 tablespoon white vinegar

¾ teaspoon salt

¼ teaspoon black pepper

¼ teaspoon red pepper flakes (optional)

1 cup olive oil

Chimichurri sauce originates from Argentina and is used as a marinade for fish, poultry, or beef. It is also often served on top of meat, used to drizzle on roasted or sautéed vegetables to add flavor, or even used as salad dressing. With so many options, this sauce is always great to have on hand.

Classic Guacamole with Kale

Serves 4 to 5.

INSTRUCTIONS:

1. Peel and pit the avocados.
2. In a bowl, mash the avocados with a fork (or chop them with a knife to keep them chunky).
3. Juice the 2 limes over the avocado and mix together. Add the remaining ingredients and fold everything together until well combined.
4. Serve with chips or use for your favorite tacos, burritos, or enchiladas.

INGREDIENTS:

3 avocados, peeled and pitted

2 limes, juiced

2 cloves garlic, minced

½ teaspoon kosher salt

1 jalapeño, seeded and chopped

¼ cup red onion, chopped

1 Roma tomato, seeded and diced

1 cup loosely packed kale leaves, finely chopped

½ cup cilantro, chopped (optional)

Kale and Pistachio Pesto

Makes 2 cups of pesto sauce.

INSTRUCTIONS:

1. Add all of the ingredients except for the oil to a blender or food processor. Pulse a few times until all ingredients are chopped. You may need to take off the lid and stir with a spoon a couple of times.
2. Leaving the processor/blender on, slowly add the olive oil and blend until a thick sauce is formed. For a thinner sauce, add more oil and/or a small amount of water until desired consistency is achieved.

INGREDIENTS:

2 cups fresh basil leaves, packed

5 cups dino kale leaves, packed

4 cloves garlic

½ cup shelled pistachios

¾ cup parmesan cheese, grated

¼ teaspoon salt

½ cup olive oil

Kale pesto is your gateway to a satisfying meal. The recipe above creates a flavor-packed sauce that can be used for pastas, pizza, paninis, and can even be used as salad dressing when you add a small amount of oil and vinegar to it. If this sauce is made with kale, and looks like kale, does that mean it tastes like kale? In a word, no. The bitter kale flavor is completely masked by delicious pesto flavor, and the texture comes out just like a regular pesto sauce. If you feel inspired to experiment, try adding various herbs like parsley, or sage!

Pico de Gallo Salsa with Kale

Makes 3 cups of salsa.

INSTRUCTIONS:

1. Add all of the ingredients to a large bowl and gently fold together. Test the salsa for flavor and add more salt and/or lime juice as desired.

2. Serve with chips, inside your favorite burrito (or burrito bowl), on top of tacos or huevos rancheros, or with anything and everything that could use a little salsa.

3. Place leftovers in a sealable container or jar and keep in the refrigerator for up to 10 days.

INGREDIENTS:

2 cups tomatoes, diced (about 4 Roma tomatoes or 2 heirloom tomatoes)

1 lime, juiced

1 cup white onion, chopped

2 jalapeños, seeded and chopped

1 cup loosely packed curly kale leaves, finely chopped

⅓ cup fresh cilantro, chopped

¼ teaspoon kosher salt, or to taste

Pineapple, Corn, and Kale Salsa

Makes 4 cups salsa.

INSTRUCTIONS:

1. Add sliced kale leaves to a large mixing bowl and drizzle the lime juice over them. Stir to coat the leaves. Allow leaves to sit about 5 minutes to allow lime juice to break down some of the fiber.
2. Add the remaining ingredients to the bowl and stir together.
3. Serve with chips, on top of tacos, or in burritos!

INGREDIENTS:

2 cups loosely packed dino kale leaves, thinly sliced

3 tablespoons lime juice

¾ cup red onion, finely chopped

2 jalapeños, seeded and finely chopped

1 ear corn, cooked, kernels removed

2 cups pineapple, chopped

1 teaspoon fresh ginger, peeled and grated

1 tablespoon cilantro leaves, finely chopped

Pinch of salt

Roasted Beet, Walnut, and Kale Pesto

Makes 1½ cups of sauce.

INSTRUCTIONS:

1. Preheat the oven to 375 degrees F.
2. Wash and scrub the beet and pat it dry. Chop it into ½" cubes and place them on a sheet of foil. Wrap the chopped beet in foil, making a foil packet. Place the packet on a baking sheet.
3. Wrap the garlic cloves (with skin still on) in foil and place on the baking sheet with the beet packet. Roast in the oven for 50 minutes, taking the garlic cloves out after 25 to 30 minutes. Allow beets and garlic to cool completely.
4. Add all ingredients except for the oil to a food processor or blender and pulse several times.
5. Leaving the food processor/blender running, slowly add the olive oil until all ingredients are well combined.
6. Use pesto for all sorts of delicious dishes, including pasta, crostini, paninis, etc.

INGREDIENTS:

1 cup beet, chopped and roasted (about 1 medium beet)

10 cloves garlic, roasted

½ cup walnuts, roasted

½ cup aged gouda cheese

1 cup tightly packed curly kale leaves

½ cup olive oil

3 tablespoons lemon juice

¼ teaspoon ground cumin

Salt to taste

For those who have never made pesto using beets, I highly recommend you try it! This sauce can be used in all the same ways as a basil pesto sauce: in pastas, on pizzas, on sandwiches or crostinis, etc. Not only is this sauce versatile, fun, and tasty but also it is incredibly nutrient-dense!

Roasted Garlic Kale Hummus

Serves 6.

INSTRUCTIONS:

1. Preheat the oven to 400 degrees F.
2. Wrap the garlic cloves (with the skin on) in aluminum foil and place in the oven to roast for 20 minutes. Allow garlic to cool before peeling the skin off.
3. Add all ingredients to a food processor and blend until smooth.
4. Serve hummus with olive oil drizzled on top and with pita bread or fresh vegetables.

INGREDIENTS:

7 cloves garlic, roasted

1 15-ounce can garbanzo beans, drained

1 cup tightly packed kale leaves

Juice of 2 lemons (¼ cup fresh lemon juice)

2 to 3 tablespoons water

¼ cup tahini paste

½ teaspoon salt, or to taste

Olive oil for serving

Tomatillo-Kale Salsa

Makes 5 cups of salsa.

INSTRUCTIONS:

1. Preheat the oven to 425 degrees F.
2. Remove the leaves from the tomatillos and cut them in half. Place them face-down on a lightly oiled or parchment-lined baking sheet. Leaving the skins on, wrap the cloves of garlic in foil and place them on the baking sheet with the tomatillos.
3. Bake until skin begins turning slightly and browned and juices are seeping out, about 12 to 15 minutes.
4. Allow the tomatillos to cool then place them in a blender or food processor. Unwrap the garlic cloves and remove the skins. Place the garlic and the remaining ingredients in the blender/processor.
5. Blend until everything is combined but still slightly chunky. Use for chips and dip, enchiladas, or various yummy dishes.

Note: You can save the salsa in the refrigerator for up to 10 days. If the salsa becomes thick/congealed after it has been refrigerated, simply add water to it and stir vigorously until a uniform consistency results.

INGREDIENTS:

12 medium to large tomatillos, roasted

8 cloves garlic, roasted

2 jalapeños, roasted

2 cups loosely packed kale leaves

1 cup white onion, chopped

½ cup tightly packed cilantro leaves

2 tablespoons fresh lime juice

1 teaspoon sugar

½ teaspoon salt

Tomatillo salsa, or "salsa verde" or "green salsa," has always been one of my favorites for eating on burritos. Adding kale makes this green salsa even greener and you can't taste the difference! You can use this salsa in the Chili Verde Shredded Chicken Enchilada recipe in this book (pg. 147), on tacos, on scrambled eggs, or do as I do and spoon-feed it to yourself.

White Bean Kale Dip

Serves 6.

INSTRUCTIONS:

1. In a blender or food processor, pulse together the first five ingredients.
2. Leaving the processor/blender on, slowly pour in the oil and lemon juice. Continue to blend until desired consistency is reached. If the dip is too thick to blend, add a small amount of water (about 1 tablespoon).
3. Serve dip with fresh vegetables, crackers, or pita bread. Also use this dip as a spread for sandwiches or paninis.

INGREDIENTS:

2 14-ounce cans cannellini beans, drained and well rinsed

3 leaves fresh sage, chopped

2 cups loosely packed kale leaves, chopped

¾ teaspoon kosher salt

2 cloves garlic, minced

4 tablespoons olive oil

3 tablespoons fresh lemon juice

Index

Brussels sprouts
    Thai Chicken Chopped Salad, 107–8
burgers
    Barbecue Black Bean, Kale, and Sweet Potato Veggie
        Burgers, 139
    Turkey Sliders with Caramelized Onions, Sautéed
        Kale, and Blue Cheese, 73
burritos
    Chicken and Kale Burrito Bowls, 145
    Sweet Potato Veggie Burritos with Coconut Curry
        Sauce, 173
Buttermilk Parsley Salad Dressing, 179
butternut squash
    Butternut Squash and Kale Chili, 113
Buttery, Crispy, Sautéed Kale Crostini with Beet and
    Kale Pesto, 57

C
cabbage
    Zesty Kale Slaw, 75
Cajun Seasoning, 141
Candied Walnuts, 93–94
cannellini beans. *see* beans, white
caponata
    Roasted Portobello Mushrooms with Eggplant
        Caponata, 171
caramelized onions
    Turkey Sliders with Caramelized Onions, Sautéed
        Kale, and Blue Cheese, 73
carrots
    Beet and Kale Slaw Salad, 83
    Minestrone Soup with Quinoa, 129
    Smoked Paprika Chicken Corn Chowder, 131
    Thai Chicken Chopped Salad, 107–8
    Zesty Kale Slaw, 75
casserole
    Creamy Portobello and Kale Quinoa Bake, 149
cauliflower
    Balsamic Roasted Vegetables with Beet Pesto Quinoa,
        51
    Cauliflower and Kale Yellow Curry, 143
    Spanish Cauliflower "Rice," 67
celery
    Kale and White Bean Soup, 127
    Minestrone Soup with Quinoa, 129
    Smoked Paprika Chicken Corn Chowder, 131
Charmoula Sauce, 181
    Eggplant, Kale, and Chickpea Tacos with Charmoula
        Sauce, 151
cheddar cheese. *see* cheese, cheddar
cheese, blue
    Roasted Beet and Fig Massaged Kale Salad, 101–2
    Turkey Sliders with Caramelized Onions, Sautéed
        Kale, and Blue Cheese, 73
cheese, cheddar

Cheddar Kale Skillet Cornbread, 61
Zucchini, Kale, and Leek Fritters with Yogurt
    Dipping Sauce, 77–78
Zucchini, Kale, and Sage Frittata, 47
cheese, feta
    Green Quinoa Salad with Asparagus, Avocado, and
        Kale Pesto, 87
    Grilled Kale, Peach, and Corn Salad, 89
    Mediterranean Quinoa and Kale Salad, 97
cheese, goat
    Massaged Kale Salad, 93–94
    Superfood Stuffed Acorn Squash, 69–70
cheese, gouda
    Creamy Portobello and Kale Quinoa Bake, 149
    Roasted Beet, Walnut, and Kale Pesto, 193
    Savory Cheesy Kale Pancakes, 43
cheese, jack
    Sausage and Kale Scramble, 41
    Southwest Stuffed Bell Peppers, 65
    Zucchini, Kale, and Sage Frittata, 47
cheese, mozzarella
    Buttery, Crispy, Sautéed Kale Crostini with Beet and
        Kale Pesto, 57
    Creamy Portobello and Kale Quinoa Bake, 149
    Sausage and Kale Scramble, 41
    Shrimp, Artichoke Heart, Sun-Dried Tomato Pesto
        Pizza, 163–64
    Turkey Sausage, Bell Pepper, Mushroom Pizza,
        153–54
cheese, parmesan
    Cheesy Mashed Yams, 55
    Creamy Portobello and Kale Quinoa Bake, 149
    Minestrone Soup with Quinoa, 129
cheese, pepper jack
    Chili Verde Shredded Chicken Enchiladas, 147
cheese, ricotta
    Creamy Portobello and Kale Quinoa Bake, 149
Cheesy Mashed Yams, 55
chevre. *see* cheese, goat
chicken
    Chicken and Kale Burrito Bowls, 145
    Chili Verde Shredded Chicken Enchiladas, 147
    Chorizo, Potato, and Kale Hash, 23
    Crock Pot Shredded Chicken Chili with Mushrooms
        and Kale, 121
    Lemony Braised Chicken and Kale, 159
    Smoked Paprika Chicken Corn Chowder, 131
    Thai Chicken Chopped Salad, 107–8
    Thai Coconut Soup with Brown Rice and Chicken,
        133
chickpeas
    Butternut Squash and Kale Chili, 113
    Eggplant, Kale, and Chickpea Tacos with Charmoula
        Sauce, 151
    Indian Chickpea Stew with Kale, 125